Newspaper Reports

by

Swami Vivekananda

Double 9 BOOKS

Newspaper Reports
by Swami Vivekananda

ISBN: 978-93-59393-70-4

Published by

DOUBLE 9 BOOKS
2/13-B, Ansari Road
Daryaganj, New Delhi – 110002
info@double9books.com
www.double9books.com
Tel. 011-40042856

ABOUT THE AUTHOR

Swami Vivekananda was born Narendranath Datta in India on January 12, 1863. He died on July 4, 1902, and was the most important student of the Indian saint Ramakrishna. He was an important part of bringing Vedanta and Yoga to the West. He is also charged with making people more aware of other religions and making Hinduism a major world religion. Vivekananda had a lot of success at the Parliament. In the years that followed, he gave hundreds of lectures across the United States, England, and Europe to spread the main ideas of Hinduism. He also started the Vedanta Society of New York and the Vedanta Society of San Francisco, which is now the Vedanta Society of Northern California. Both of these groups became the basis for Vedanta Societies in the West. Vivekananda was one of the most important philosophers and social reformers in India at the time. He was also one of the most successful and powerful Vedanta missionaries in the West.People now think of him as one of the most important people in modern India and Hinduism. Mahatma Gandhi said that after reading Vivekananda's works, he loved his country a thousand times more.

CONTENTS

Response To Welcome*

(New Discoveries, Vol. 1, pp. 83-84.)

[Editorial synthesis of four Chicago newspaper reports from:

Herald, Inter Ocean, Tribune, *and* Record,

ca. September 11, 1893]

[Sisters and Brothers of America,]

It fills my heart with joy unspeakable to rise in response to the grand words of welcome given to us by you. I thank you in the name of the most ancient order of monks the world has ever seen, of which Gautama was only a member. I thank you in the name of the Mother of religions, of which Buddhism and Jainism are but branches; and I thank you, finally, in the name of the millions and millions of Hindoo people of all castes and sects. My thanks also to some of the speakers on the platform who have told you that these different men from far-off nations will bear to the different lands the idea of toleration which they may see here. My thanks to them for this idea.

I am proud to belong to a religion which has taught the world both tolerance and universal acceptance. We believe not only in universal tolerance but we accept all religions to be true. I am proud to tell you that I belong to a religion in whose sacred language, the Sanskrit, the word exclusion is untranslatable. (Applause) I am proud to belong to a nation which has sheltered the persecuted and the refugees of all religions and all nations of the earth. I am proud to tell you that we have gathered in our bosom the purest remnant of the Israelites, a remnant of which came to southern India and took refuge with us in the very years in which their holy temple was shattered to pieces by Roman tyranny. I am proud to belong to the religion which has sheltered and is still fostering the remnant of the grand Zoroastrian nation.

I will quote to you, brothers, a few lines from a hymn which every Hindoo child repeats every day. I feel that the very spirit of this hymn, which I remember to have repeated from my earliest boyhood, which is every day repeated by millions and millions of men in India, has at last come to be realized. "As the different streams, having their sources in different places, all mingle their water in the sea; O Lord, so the different paths which men take through different tendencies, various though they appear, crooked or straight, all lead to Thee."

The present convention, which is one of the most august assemblies ever held, is in itself an indication, a declaration to the world of the wonderful doctrine preached in the *Gita*: "Whosoever comes to Me, through whatsoever form I reach him, all are struggling through paths that in the end always lead to me." Sectarianism, bigotry and its horrible descendant fanaticism, have possessed long this beautiful earth. It has filled the earth with violence, drenched it often and often with human gore, destroyed civilization and sent whole nations into despair. But its time has come, and I fervently believe that the bell that tolled this morning in honor of the representatives of the different religions of the earth, in this parliament assembled, is the death-knell to all fanaticism (applause), that it is the death-knell to all persecution with the sword or the pen, and to all uncharitable feelings between brethren wending their way to the same goal, but through different ways.

Parlor Talk*

(New Discoveries.)

[*Chicago Record,* September 11, 1893]

Four leaders of religious thought were sitting in Dr. Barrow's [Barrows's] parlor — the Jain, George Condin [Candlin], the missionary who has passed sixteen years in China, Swami Vivekananda, the learned Brahman (The Swami was a Kshatriya, not a Brahmin.) Hindoo, and Dr. John H. Barrows, the Chicago Presbyterian. These four talked as if they were brothers of one faith.

The Hindoo is of smooth countenance. His rather fleshy face is bright and intelligent. He wears an orange turban and a robe of the same color. His English is very good. "I have no home," said he.

> I travel about from one college to another in India, lecturing to the students. Before starting for America I had been for some time in Madras. Since arriving in this country I have been treated with utmost courtesy and kindness. It is very gratifying to us to be recognized in this Parliament, which may have such an important bearing on the religious history of the world. We expect to learn much and take back some great truths to our 15,000,000 faithful Brahmins.

Religion Not The Crying Need Of India*

(*New Discoveries*, Vol. 1, pp. 123-26.)

[A verbatim transcript of the address, delivered at the Parliament of Religions, September 20, 1893]

[*Chicago Inter Ocean*, September 21, 1893]

Swami Vivekananda

At the close of the reading of Mr. Headland's paper on "Religion in Peking" Dr. Momerie announced that the other speakers bulletined for the evening had failed to appear. It was but 9 o'clock, and the main auditorium and galleries were well filled. There was an outburst of applause as they caught sight of the Hindoo monk, Vivekananda, sitting in his orange robe and scarlet turban upon the platform.

This popular Hindoo responded to the generous applause by saying that he did not come to speak to-night. He took occasion, however, to criticise many of the statements made in the paper by Mr. Headland. Referring to the poverty which prevails in China, he said that the missionaries would do better to work in appeasing hunger than in endeavoring to persuade the Chinese to renounce their faith of centuries and embrace Christianity at [as] the price of food. And then the Hindu stepped back on the platform and whispered to Bishop Keane, of the Catholic church, a moment.

He then resumed his address by saying that Bishop Keane had told him that Americans would not be offended at honest criticism. He said he had heard of all the terrible things and horrible conditions which prevail in China but he had not heard that any asylums had been erected by Christians for remedying all these difficulties. He said:

> Christian brethren of America, you are so fond of sending out missionaries to save the souls of heathens. I ask you what have you done and are doing to save their bodies from starvation? (Applause). In India, there are 300,000,000 men and women living on an average of a little more than 50 cents a month. I have seen them living for years upon wild flowers. Whenever there was a little famine hundreds of thousands died of starvation. Christian missionaries come and offer life but only on condition that the Hindoos become Christians, abandoning the faith of their fathers and

forefathers. Is it right? There are hundreds of asylums, but if the Mohammedans or the Hindoos go there they would be kicked out. There are thousands of asylums erected by Hindoos where anybody would be received. There are hundreds of churches that have been erected with the assistance of the Hindoos, but no Hindoo temples for which a Christian has given a penny.

What the East Needs

> Brethren of America, the crying evil of the East is not religion. We have more than religion enough; what they want is bread, but they are given a stone. (Applause). It is an insult to a suffering man dying of hunger to preach to him metaphysics. Therefore, if you wish to illustrate the meaning of "brotherhood" treat the Hindoo more kindly, even though he be a Hindoo and is faithful to his religion. Send missionaries to them to teach them how better to earn a better piece of bread and not to teach them metaphysical nonsense. (Great applause).

And then the monk said he was in ill health today and wished to be excused. But there were thunders of applause and cries of "Go on" and Mr. Vivekananda continued.

> The paper just read says something about the miserable and ignorant priest. The same may be said of India. I am one of those monks who have been described as beggarly. That is the pride of my life. (Applause). I am proud in that sense to be Christ-like. I eat what I have today and think not of tomorrow. "Behold the lilies of the field; they toil not, neither do they spin." The Hindoo carries that out literally. Many gentlemen present in Chicago sitting on this platform can testify that for the last twelve years I never knew whence my next meal was coming. I am proud to be a beggar for the sake of the Lord. The idea in the east is [that] to preach or teach anything for the sake of money is low and vulgar, but to teach the name of the Lord for pay is such a degradation as would cause the priest to lose caste and be spat upon. There is one suggestion in the paper that is true: If the priests of China and India were organized there is an enormous amount of potential energy which could be used for regeneration of society and humanity. I endeavored to organize it in India, but failed for lack of money. It may be I shall get the help I want in America.
>
> But we know it is very hard for a heathen to get any help from "Christian people". (Great applause). I have heard

> so much of this land of freedom, of liberty and freedom of thought that I am not discouraged. I thank you, ladies and gentlemen.

And then the popular visitor bowed gracefully and sought to retire with a graceful smile, but the audience cried to him to proceed. Mr. Vivekananda, fairly bubbling with an expression of good nature, then explained the Hindoo theory of [re]incarnation. At the close of the address Dr. Momerie [a delegate from England] said that he now understood why the newspapers had well called this parliament an approach to the millennium. . . .

The Chicago Letter

(*New Discoveries*, Vol. 1, pp. 162-63.)

[*New York Critic*, November 11, 1893]

. . .It was an outgrowth of the Parliament of Religions, which opened our eyes to the fact that the philosophy of the ancient creeds contains much beauty for the moderns. When we had once clearly perceived this, our interest in their exponents quickened, and with characteristic eagerness we set out in pursuit of knowledge. The most available means of obtaining it, after the close of the Parliament, was through the addresses and lectures of Suami Vivekananda, who is still in this city. His original purpose in coming to this country was to interest Americans in the starting of new industries among the Hindoos, but he has abandoned this for the present, because he finds that, as "the Americans are the most charitable people in the world," every man with a purpose comes here for assistance in carrying it out. When asked about the relative condition of the poor here and in India, he replied that our poor would be princes there, and that he had been taken through the worst quarter of the city only to find it, from the standpoint of his knowledge, comfortable and even pleasant.

A Brahmin of the Brahmins, Vivekananda gave up his rank to join the brotherhood of monks, where all pride of caste is voluntarily relinquished. And yet he bears the mark of race upon his person. His culture, his eloquence, and his fascinating personality have given us a new idea of Hindoo civilization. He is an interesting figure, his fine, intelligent, mobile face in its setting of yellows, and his deep, musical voice prepossessing one at once in his favor. (The Swami quoted this passage in his letter to Shri Haridas Viharidas Desai, written November 15, 1893 (Vide Complete Works, VIII: 327).) So it is not strange that he has been taken up by the literary clubs, has preached and lectured in churches, until the life of Buddha and the doctrines of his faith have grown familiar to us. He speaks without notes, presenting his facts and his conclusions with the greatest art, the most convincing sincerity; and rising at times to a rich, inspiring eloquence. As learned and cultivated, apparently, as the most accomplished Jesuit, he has also something Jesuitical in the character of his mind; but though the little sarcasms thrown into his discourses are as keen as a rapier, they are so delicate as to be lost on many of his hearers. Nevertheless his courtesy is unfailing, for these thrusts are never pointed so directly at our customs as to be rude. At present he contents himself with enlightening us in regard to his religion and the words of its philosophers. He looks forward to the time when we shall pass beyond idolatry — now necessary in his opinion to the ignorant classes, — beyond worship, even, to a knowledge of the presence of God in nature, of the divinity and responsibility of man. "Work out your own salvation," he says with the dying Buddha; "I cannot help you. No man can help you. Help yourself."

Religions Of India

(*New Discoveries*, Vol. 1, p. 191.)

Viva Kananda, the Hindoo Orator Delivers an Interesting Lecture

(Of which there is no verbatim transcript available. Cf. Complete Works, III: 481 *for a less comprehensive report of the same lecture.*)

[*Daily Cardinal*, University of Wisconsin at Madison, November 21, 1893]

A crowded house greeted Viva Kananda at the Congregational Church last evening. The speaker was attired in native costume, which consisted of a cream turban, with yellow gown and cardinal sash.

The first part of the lecture was devoted to illustrating the many resemblances of Sanscrit [*sic*], the language of the Hindoos, to that of English. They have no word in their language which means salvation; to them it is freedom from bondage. They believe that man's real nature is perfect, and that cause and effect controls all except God. Religion was aptly illustrated by the story of the blind men who each felt of a portion of a huge elephant, and each thought the animal like the particular part he felt of it; so with religion each of the various sects have a part of the whole truth, while truth itself is infinite and no man can say "I have seen it all."

The Hindoo belief was shown to be one of the most charitable of beliefs. Persecution is something unknown in India; there is no such word in their language. The lecturer challenged the world to show an instance in Hindoo progress, of a Christian missionary being persecuted. A Greek historian, writing of them said: "No Hindoo man is dishonest, no Hindoo woman unchaste."

Viva Kananda came to this country from India in the interest of the world's congress of religions, and his lecture last evening on the "Religions of India," was an inspiration to all who heard him. He has a pleasant, clear-cut, dusky face, and a decidedly impressive manner and bearing. His voice is low and pleasant, with a secret something which rivets your attention at the start.

All Religions Are True Such Is The Message Brought From India

BY A HINDU MONK

(*New Discoveries*, Vol. 1, pp. 200-202.)

[*Daily Iowa Capitol*, November 28, 1893]

SWAMI VIVEKANANDA TELLS OF ANCIENT FAITH

SPEAKS AGAIN TONIGHT

(The lecture was "The Hindu Religion", delivered November 27, 1893, of which there is no verbatim transcript available. Cf. Complete Works, III: 482-84 for different highlights of the same lecture.)

It was a rare as well as an odd treat which the people of Des Moines enjoyed last evening at the Central Church of Christ. A monk, of the ancient faith of Brahma, made a happy presentation of that faith, not so much of its peculiarities as of its underlying principles. The audience was a good sized one, perhaps 500 or 600 persons being present. The main floor being well filled and there were perhaps a couple of hundred in the gallery.

The speaker opened by saying that all religious systems were an attempt to answer the question What am I? This and the kindred ones, Whence Come I? and Whither Am I Going? are constantly recurring. Without following the speaker throughout the entire lecture, suffice it to say, that underlying the Hindu religion according to the speaker is the belief that "We are all divine". In each is a conscious spirit that survives the body and the mind and is a part of the absolute. The speaker very ably defended religion against the attacks of science. The latter can use only the five senses, and unless a thing can be proven to be by these senses [it] is disposed to doubt its existence. But does science know that there are only five senses? The speaker contended for the existence of a supersensuous sense; through which man obtains revelations of spiritual truths. The Hindu word for revelation is "Veda". Hence the "Vedas" are the revelations. These writings are not confined to those of the Hindus, but include those of all peoples; because said the speaker, all religions are true.

When "revelations" undertake to tell of material things they enter upon a domain which belongs to science and are not to be accepted. There was an ancient superstition that because Moses gave a revelation of the will of God, therefore everything Moses wrote must be true. There is a modern superstition that, because there are mistakes in the writings of Moses, therefore nothing Moses wrote is true. When Moses wrote the tables of the law he was inspired. When he told of the creation what he said was merely the speculations of Moses the Jew.

The speaker was not favorably impressed with the efforts to make Hindu converts — perverts he calls them — to Christianity, nor the converse. All religions being true, such perversions serve no good end. The Hindu religion the speaker claimed is not disposed to antagonize any belief; it absorbs them. As for tolerating different beliefs, the language of the Hindu has no word corresponding with the English word "intolerance". That language had a word for religion and one for sect. The former embraced all beliefs. The conception of the latter the speaker illustrated by telling the story of the frog, who had no idea there was any world outside the well in which he had always lived.

The speaker urged his hearers to cultivate the divine within them and to discard the "nonsense" of sects.

The lecturer is an able, dignified and forcible speaker. His mastery of English is perfect, there being only the faintest indications of a foreign accent. The lecturer was followed with closest attention by the audience. After the lecture, the speaker consented to answer questions to a portion of the audience that remained for that purpose. In the course of the answers he said that the Hindus were altogether opposed to the destruction of the life of any animal. He admitted the worship of the sacred cow. He said further that the Hindus had nothing answering to our church organizations. He was his own priest, bishop and pope. . . .

A Message From India

(*New Discoveries*, Vol. 1, pp. 204-6.)

Vive Kananda, the Famous Hindoo Monk and Scholar,

Appears in Des Moines

[*Iowa State Register*, November 28, 1893]

A YOUNG MAN OF THIRTY YEARS

AND A BIG, ACTIVE BRAIN AND TRUE HEART

The people of Des Moines had a glimpse of Oriental life and thought at its best yesterday, from the lips of the famous Hindoo monk, Swami Vive Kananda. A central figure in the great Parliament of Religions at Chicago this summer, where he coped with some of the greatest minds of the country with honor to himself and his people, he gave those who heard him, and especially those who met him at Dr. Breeden's, something new to think about. It was a message from over the sea, from another people of wholly different surroundings, training, customs and traditions, but as the monk says, the basic principles are the same in all religions. It is his doctrine that there is good in all religions and he preaches it with great power. . . .

Yesterday afternoon he met a large number of the brightest women in Des Moines, members of the various literary clubs, at the invitation of Mrs. H. O. Breeden, at her home, 1318 Woodland avenue, (An informal talk of which there is no verbatim transcript available.) and he talked to them for two or three hours about his religion, his view of Christianity, in which he heartily concurs, and of the manners and customs of his people. The thing which Vive Kananda most strongly insists upon is that the Hindoo religion is not to be blamed for all that is bad in India any more than Christianity is to be blamed for all that is bad in America. And he insists that it is absurd to give Christianity credit for all the marvelous undertakings and achievements of the people who cherish it. He joins in the praise of the sublime things in the bible [*sic*], but says that when Moses undertook to speak of the creation of the world, he was merely Moses, the Jew and nothing more.

This view from the other side, and a sympathetic side at that, is a most helpful and instructive and intensely interesting one. Vive Kananda uses the purest English, for he was well educated in the English university, Calcutta.

He praises the American women most enthusiastically.

> I do not know what would have become of me if it had not been for your women,

he said to a reporter for *The Register* last night.

> They took me up and took care of me and made all necessary arrangements for me. They are the best women in the world. They have been so kind to me,

[the Swami said] with a grateful smile.

. . . . . .

Reincarnation*

(*New Discoveries*, Vol. 1, p. 206-7.)

[*Daily Iowa Capitol*, November 29, 1893]

Swami Vivekananda last night talked of reincarnation. (Of which there is no verbatim transcript available.) It is based, he contended, on the fact that there never has been a new creation; that creation has existed coevally with God from all eternity. Departed souls find bodies to inhabit either better or worse than their former tenement, according as they made them fit for one or the other. The lecturer will speak again on Thanksgiving evening at the same place on the manners and customs of India.

An Intellectual Feast

(*New Discoveries*, Vol. 1, p. 208.)

[*Iowa State Register*, November 30, 1893]

The remarkable discussions started by the famous Hindu monk, Vive Kananda, were the topic of interest in intellectual circles yesterday. Especially so was his comment on the work of American missionaries in India, and his strong defense of his own people and morals and religion. His position is that the people of India do not need any more religion, but training in the practical things of life that will enable them to cope with the English who have occupied India. Vive Kananda was the guest of Mr. F. W. Lehman and Mr. O. H. Perkins yesterday and in their company visited the state house, which he very much admired. He took a special interest in the portraits of the American Indians that he saw there. . . .

A Prayer Meeting*

(*New Discoveries*, Vol. 1, p. 207.)

[*Des Moines Daily News*, November 30, 1893]

Vivekananda attended a prayer meeting Wednesday evening and witnessed the baptism of two young women. The service impressed him very much. He said:

> I see. The sentiment is ennobling and the ceremony beautiful. It is the more impressive that the minister is honest, earnest and believes what he says.

On American Women*

(*New Discoveries*, Vol. 1, p. 208.)

[*Daily Iowa Capitol*, November 30, 1893]

The now celebrated Hindu monk, Swami Vivekananda will lecture for the last time in Des Moines tonight. He will speak on "Life in India" ["Manners and Customs of India"] a most interesting theme. The renowned Hindu is a brilliant man about 30 years old. He says American women are lovely, but American men are entirely too practical.

On The Brahmo Samaj*

(*New Discoveries*, Vol. 1, p. 215.)

[*Iowa State Register*, December 1, 1893]

Before he left the city [Des Moines, Iowa], Vive Kananda took occasion to say a warm word of praise for the Bramo-Somaj [*sic*], the work it is doing in India, especially for the women, and of its representative in this country. The visit of Vive Kananda, stirring as it did the intellectual centers of the city to their depths and starting a lively religious discussion, prepared the way for the present visitor [Nagarkar] from the Orient and heightened public interest in whatever he might have to say.

A Witty Hindu

(*New Discoveries*, Vol. 1, pp. 216-17.)

[*Minneapolis Journal*, December 15, 1893]

SWAMI VIVEKANANDA

ENTERTAINS ANOTHER LARGE AUDIENCE

A large number of people assembled at the Unitarian church last evening for the purpose of listening to Swami Vivekananda of India. The customs and manners of the people of that country were described, (The lecture was "The Manners and Customs of India", of which there is no verbatim transcript available. Cf. the following American newspaper report, "The Manners and Customs of India", for other highlights of the lecture.) and during his lecture the Brahmin took occasion to show up some of the rough points of America. He is of the humorist order and his quick replies and witty sallies rarely failed to evoke applause. He would not admit that his people were wrong in everything, but there were a great many things peculiar to India which the Americans did not approve of and yet which might be all right. He had never seen husband and wife go before a magistrate to tell their troubles. They grew up with the idea that they were to be married and they loved each other as brothers and sisters.

He described the customs of his country, the temples, the art of the juggler and all of the other peculiarities of oriental countries in a manner that was charming. Following the address a number of questions were asked by persons in the audience.

The Manners And Customs Of India*

(*New Discoveries*, Vol. 1, pp. 217-19.)

[*Minneapolis Tribune*, December 15, 1893]

Swami Vive Kananda, the Brahmin priest, was greeted by a packed house last evening at the First Unitarian Church, when he appeared before his second Minneapolis audience. Vive Kananda is a bright, quick witted talker, ready at all points to attack or defend, and inserts a humor into his speeches that is not lost upon his auditors. He spoke last evening under the auspices of the Kappa Kappa Gammas of the University, and the audience embraced a large number of earnest thinking men and women, pleased to be enlightened upon the "Manners and Customs of India," which was his chosen subject. (Of which there is no verbatim transcript available. Cf. the preceding American newspaper report, "A witty Hindu", for other highlights of the lecture.)

Robed in his native garb, with his hands for the most part clasped behind his back, Kananda paces back and forth the narrow platform, talking as he paces, with long pauses between his sentences, as if willing that his words should sink into the deepest soil. His talk is not so weighty that the frivolous mind may not appreciate some of his sayings, but he also speaks a philosophy that carries gravest truth. He tells of the manners and customs of India, of the divided life between the male and female, of the reverence for and holiness of women, and again of their degeneracy; of the calm and peaceful life, that yet is not true life because it is not liberty; he speaks of the Mohammedans, who form one-fifth of the Indian population, and that 65,000,000, equal to the entire population of the United States. He describes the magnificence of the temples, the art of the jugglers, who are the gypsies of the Indian race, and he touches upon the superstitions of the people, of how they fill the water jars and stand them in the doorway before starting on a journey; he speaks of the metaphysical knowledge of the plowman, who yet only knows that he "pays taxes to the government"; he admits the reverence of the Hindu for the river Ganges, and his ever lingering wish that he shall die on its banks; he tells all these things in a quiet, half supercilious voice that presently leads to some remark on the American way of doing things, and then his audience is in a ripple of laughter, and a tremor of clapping expresses amused acknowledgement of his sarcasm. . . .

When some one at the close of his lecture asked him "What class of people are reached and converted by the missionaries?" he quickly replied, "You know as much about that, the American sees the reports, we never do", he has turned the query into a cause for smiling, and while the house regains its composure he paces quietly to and fro. The address was followed with the closest attention and was supplemented by several questions and answers among the audience, from whom he invited interrogation.

Hindu Philosophy

(*New Discoveries*, Vol. 1, pp. 366-69.)

[*Detroit Tribune*, February 18, 1894]

ITS RECENT EXPRESSION BY VIVE KANANDA.

HIS MISSION WORTHY THE SERIOUS ATTENTION

OF AMERICANS.

THE TWO REMARKABLE THINGS
IN THE UNITED STATES

WHICH GRATIFIES THE DISTINGUISHED
PAGAN — WHAT

ENVIRONMENT WILL DO FOR
ANY PEOPLE — RAP AT

MISSIONARIES.

There has seldom been such a sensation in cultured circles in Detroit, as that created by the advent of Swami Vive Kananda, the learned Hindu monk, whose exceptional command of our own language has enabled us to receive impressions concerning ourselves from an oriental standpoint and to acquire knowledge of a people of whose peculiar civilization and philosophy we have heard so much.

Both in public and private the Hindu brother has talked freely and frankly. He acknowledges that the masses in India are very poor, very ignorant and are divided into a diversity of sects, with forms of worship varying from downright idolatry to the broadest and most liberal form of divine conception based on the brotherhood of man and the oneness of God. His mission, he says, is not to proselyte us — to try and make us think as he does — but to get means to start a college in India for the education of teachers who are to go among the common people and work a reform of existing evils, of which there are many. He states that India is priest-ridden to a harrowing degree. It is priest-craft that distorts truth and perpetuates ignorance. It is priest-craft that substitutes its own crude and narrow interpretations for truth, which perverts the people and prevents their moral progression. The Swami regards all sects and creeds from a broad basis. He even sees good in idolatry. It is an ideal, he thinks, for the ignorant whose mental capacity is insufficient to grasp abstract ideas, and who require a direct personification in some material form. He frankly states that we of the occident are also retarded in our progression by too much priest-craft, and that we are not free from idolatrous practices, in that some of our sects worship shrines, figures and pictures and even the sanctity with which the rostrum and pulpit of a modern church is regarded is an ideal idolatry.

Two Remarkable Things in This Country

The Swami notes two most remarkable things in this country, when asked his frank opinion of us: First, the superiority of our women, as regards influence in position and intellect. Second, in our charities and treatment of the poor, he says, we have almost solved the problem as to what shall be done with them. Not only in this, in the direction of hospitals and charitable institutions, but in our tremendous development of labor-saving machinery. He has no admiration for our material progress, as it does not make man better, nor for our boasted civilization, as we only ape and imitate the customs and manners of the English — sometimes to a very ridiculous extent. We are yet too young, to have a distinctive civilization; we have yet to assimilate the human sewerage of Europe we have allowed to be poured upon us, before we produce a distinct American type.

[The writer goes on to say that the Swami's Indian background makes it difficult for him to understand that Western competitiveness is not undesirable but a primal law of nature itself — the survival of the fittest — and that inasmuch as "the dreamy and sentimental philosophy of the Hindoos" accounts for their poverty, degradation, and domination by a "mere handful of Englishmen," the Swami would do well neither to ignore nor to despise the materialism of the West. Having thus editorialized, he continues:]

His Criticism of Missionaries

If what he states is true about the results accomplished by foreign missions in India, the various boards of these various organizations would do well to consult him and follow his advice. It is for the betterment of his people he is here. But he says missionary work does no good; only adds additional sects and creeds to an already sect-ridden country; that the teachings of the Vedas, with which every Hindoo is familiar, is identical with the teachings of Christ. He makes the reasonable plea that foreign creeds and dogmas are not consonant with their inherited proclivities or civilization, and are consequently difficult to propagate.

The mission of Kananda is, however, one that should commend it[self] to every lover of humanity. He hopes to see the best of our material philosophy and progress infused into Hindoo civilization, and that, also, we may take lessons from them, until we shall all become, as we once were in ages past, brother Aryans, possessing a common civilization — the exalted philosophy of non-self, being alike without sect or creed in oneness with God.

FRED H. SEYMOUR.

A GOD EVERY DAY

[*Detroit Tribune*, February 19, 1894]

RABBI GROSSMAN IS REFRESHED
BY SWAMI VIVE KANANDA

. . . "I take your Jesus," Kananda said last Saturday evening [February 17]. (Vide *"The Divinity of Man"* (Complete Works, III: 496-501*) and "Is India a Benighted Country?"* (Complete Works, IV: 198-202).)

> I take him to my heart as I take all the great and good of all lands and of all times. But you, will you take my Krishna to your heart? No — you cannot, you dare not — still you are the cultured and I am the heathen. . . .

Vive Kananda Leaves

(*New Discoveries*, Vol. 1, p. 380.)

[*Detroit Journal*, February 23, 1894]

HE TELLS SOMETHING

ABOUT THE CONDITIONS OF HINDOO LABORERS.

Swami Vive Kananda repaid the admiration of his lady acquaintances by writing verses, at the same time religious and semi-sentimental, yesterday afternoon. He departed this morning for Ada, O. [Ohio].

In a conversation concerning the material condition of the Hindu workingmen, the learned monk said that the poor lived on porridge alone. The laborer ate a breakfast of porridge, went off to his daily toil and returned in the evening to another breakfast of porridge and called it dinner. In most of the provinces the farmers were so poor that they could not afford to eat any of the wheat raised. A day laborer on a farm received only 12 pence a day, but a dollar in India brought 10 times as much as it would in this country. Cotton was raised, but its fiber was so short it had to be woven by hand, and even then it was necessary to import American and Egyptian cotton to mix with it.

Culture At Home

(*New Discoveries*, Vol. 1, p. 365.)

[*Detroit Evening News*, February 25, 1894]

ANECDOTES OF SWAMI VIVE
KANANDA'S VISIT TO DETROIT.

Anecdotes of Swami Vive Kananda's visit are numerous and amusing — at least they must have been amusing to him, although a little humiliating to the American self-love. One lady said:

"I really was ashamed at the contrast between the knowledge possessed by him and by some of our Detroit men who consider themselves gentlemen of culture. At one dinner party a gentleman asked Kananda what books he would advise him to read on chemistry, whereupon the Hindu monk responded with a long list of English works on this science, which one would naturally expect an American to know more about than a Hindu. Another gentleman followed by a request as to books on astronomy, to which Kananda obligingly answered with another equally good list of English astronomical works. But his growing astonishment reached its climax when a lady spoke of 'The Christ,' and said, 'What do those words mean?' He again furnished the desired information, but in a tone growing slightly sarcastic."

Probably the choicest example of nineteenth century civilization and culture was given by a lady, who asked Kananda if he liked the English. He very naturally responded that he did not. Then she continued, with fine tact, to pursue the subject still further by touching references to that pleasant event, the Sepoy rebellion. As the Hindu grew excited she smiled at him ironically and said:

"I thought I could disturb your philosophical Eastern calm."

Kananda, The Pagan

(*New Discoveries*, Vol. 1, pp. 410-16.)

[*Detroit Tribune*, March 11, 1894]

ATTACKED CHRISTIAN MISSIONS
IN LAST NIGHT'S LECTURE.

AND HIS WORDS WERE WARMLY APPLAUDED

BY THE AUDIENCE.

CHRISTIAN NATIONS KILL AND
MURDER, HE SAID, AND IMPORT

DISEASE INTO FOREIGN COUNTRIES,
THEN ADD INSULT TO

INJURY BY PREACHING OF A CRUCIFIED CHRIST.

Swami Vive Kananda lectured to a very large audience at the Detroit Opera House last night on "Christian Missions in India.", (Cf. "Christianity in India", Complete Works, VIII: 214-9, for a somewhat less comprehensive report of the same lecture.) One could believe that the lecture was intended as an answer to the many statements of missionaries which have been aimed at Kananda during the past two weeks in this city.

Kananda was introduced by Honorable Thomas W. Palmer last night, who recited a fable by way of preface. "Two knights of honor once met on the field," he said, "and seeing a shield hanging on a tree they halted. One said: 'What a very fine silver shield.' The other replied that it was not silver but copper. Each disputed the other's statement until at last they got off their horses, tied them to the tree, and drawing their swords fought for several hours. After they were both well spent by the loss of blood they staggered against each other and fell on the opposite sides from where they had been fighting. Then one glanced up at the pendant shield and said: 'You were right, my friend. The shield is copper.' The other looked up and said: 'It is I who was mistaken. The shield is silver.' If they had looked at both sides of the shield in the first place it would have saved the loss of much blood. I think that if we looked at both sides of every question there would be less argument and fighting.

"We have with us tonight a gentleman who, from the christian standpoint is, I suppose, a pagan. But he belongs to a religion which was old long before ours was thought of by men. I am sure that it will be pleasant to hear from the copper side of the shield. We have looked at it only from the silver side. Ladies and Gentlemen, Swami Vive Kananda."

Kananda, who had remained seated on the stage during Mr. Palmer's remarks, stepped to the front, clad in the orange robe and unique turban of the Brahman [*sic*] priest, bowed in acknowledgement of the welcoming applause, and launched at once into his subject.

What India Is

> [The Swami said:]
>
> I do not know about the efforts of christian missionaries in China and Japan except through reading the books and literature on the subject, but I can speak about the efforts of christianizing India. But before I go into this I want to place before you an idea of what India is.

Then he explained in detail how the 300,000,000 inhabitants of India are divided into castes, between which there can be no affiliation, how the natives of the south cannot understand the language of the ones of the north, and vice versa. He told how the lower caste lived on the flesh of dead animals, and never bathed their bodies, and how impossible it would be for the higher class to mingle with them, although they were granted the protection of the same laws.

He referred to the first appearance of the christians in an attempt to evangelize the followers of Buddah [Buddha]. They were Spaniards, he said, and they discovered a temple near Ceylon, in which was presented a tooth of Buddah as a sacred relic. "The Spaniard christians thought that their God commanded them to go and fight and kill and murder," he said,

> and so they seized the tooth of Buddah and destroyed it. By the way, it was not a tooth of Buddah at all, but a relic manufactured by the priests — it was a foot long. (Laughter)
>
> Every religion has its miracles; you needn't laugh because the tooth was a foot long. Well, after the Spaniards took away the tooth they converted a few hundred and killed a few thousands; and there Spain stops in the history of missionary efforts among the Buddhists.

The Portugese [*sic*] christians, he said, discovered the great temple at Bombay, built in the form of a body with three heads, in representation of the trinity as the Hindoo believes in a trinity.

"The Portugese saw it and couldn't explain it," said Kananda, with a sarcastic ring in his voice,

> and so they concluded that it was of the devil, and gathered their forces and knocked off the three heads of the temple. The devil is such a handy man. I am sorry to see him so fast disappearing.

Then Kananda outlined the various stages of christian evangelization in India, and paid very high tribute to two or three missionaries, who, he said, had been great exceptions to the rule, and lived among the people to uplift and minister to their needs.

Antagonize Native Interests

The Hindoo priest told how as soon as the land came into possession of the English people every village had its white colony, which huddled itself together and withdrew from all association with the natives. Then when the missionaries reached the country, he said, they would naturally go at once among the English people, who sympathized with them and with whom they could converse. The missionaries know nothing of the native language, he says, and so they cannot dwell with the people. Most of them are married and for the sake of getting their wives into the English society they identify themselves with all their interests, and in doing so directly antagonize the interests of the natives, and make it impossible to get in touch with them.

"We sometimes have famines in India," he said.

> And so the young missionaries will hang about the fag end of a famine and give a starving native 5 shillings, and there you have him, a ready-made christian; take him. That was probably a baptist missionary, and so when a methodist missionary comes along he gives the same native 5 shillings, and his name is again registered as a convert. The only band of converts around each missionary is composed of those dependent upon him for a living. They have to be christians or starve. And they are dwindling as the money supply decreases. I am glad if you want to make christians in India by giving work and bread to the poor. God speed you to do that. There is one benefit that must be credited to the missionary movement. It makes education cheap. The missionaries bring some money with them from the people who send them, and the Indian government appropriates some, so that there are some very good colleges and schools available to the natives through missionaries. But I will be frank with you. There are no conversions from the schools

to the christian religion. The Hindoo boy is very clever. He takes the bait, but never gets the hook.

The speaker said that the lady missionary goes into certain houses, gets four shillings a month, reads the Bible, while the native girls give indifferent attention, and teaches them to knit while they pay very keen attention. The girls, like the boys, he said are always alert to learn practical things, but they will give little heed to the christian religion, although they will espouse it if necessary to get the other advantages.

Most Missionaries Incompetent

"The most of the men whom you send us as missionaries are incompetent," he said.

> I have never known of a single man who has studied Sanscrit [*sic*] before going to India as a missionary and yet all our books and literature are printed in it.

He suggested as an explanation of the visits of the missionaries that "perhaps the atheism and scepticism at home is pushing the missionaries out all over the world." When in India he said he had thought the sole business of christianity [was] to send all people to the fires of hell, but since coming to America he has found that there are a great many liberal men. He referred to the parliament of religions, and told how a certain editor of a presbyterian paper had written an article at the close of the parliament entitled "The Lying Hindoo," in which he had scored him very severely.

In the article the editor said that "while in the parliament he was here as our guest, but now that it is over we ought to make an enthusiastic attack against him and his false doctrines."

In referring to the medical missionaries in India Kananda said:

> India requires health, but it must be health for people. And how can you help our people if you do not get in touch with them? When you come to us as missionaries you ought to throw over all idea of nationality. Jesus didn't go about among the English officials attending champagne suppers. He didn't care to have his wife get into high European society. If your missionary does not follow Christ what right has he to call himself a christian? We want missionaries of Christ. Let such come to India by the hundreds and thousands. Bring Christ's life to us and let it permeate the very core of society. Let Him be preached in every village and corner of India. But don't have your missionaries choose their profession as a means of livelihood. Let them have the call of Christ. Let them feel within that they were born for that work.
>
> As far as converting India to christianity is concerned, there is no hope. If it were possible it ought not to be done. It

would be dangerous; it would mark the destruction of all religions. If the whole universe should come to have the same temperament, physical or mental, destruction would immediately result. Why couldn't you convert the Jew? Why couldn't you make the Persians christians? Why is it that to every African who becomes a christian 100 become followers of Mohammed? Why can't you make an impression on India and China, and Japan? Because oneness of mental temperament all over the world would be death. Nature is too wise to allow such things.

Filled the World with Bloodshed

> [The Swami said:]
>
> The christian nations have filled the world with bloodshed and tyranny. It is their day now. You kill and murder and bring drunkenness and disease in our country, and then add insult to injury by preaching Christ and Him crucified. What christian voice goes through the land protesting against such horrors? I have never heard any. You drink the idea in your mothers' milk that you are angels and we are devils. It is not enough that there be sunlight; you must have the eyes to see it. It is not only necessary that there be goodness in people; you must have the appreciation of goodness within yourselves in order to distinguish it. This is in every heart until it has been murdered by superstition and hideous blasphemy.

Then Kananda drew a very beautiful simile to illustrate that the essential truths of all religions are [the] same, and all else is but incidental and unimportant environment. He told how the savage man might find a few jewels, and prizing them, tie them with a rude thong and string them about his neck. As he became slightly civilized he would perhaps exchange the thong for a string. Becoming still more enlightened he would fasten his jewels with a silken cord; and when possessed of a high civilization he would make an elaborate gold setting for his treasures. But throughout all the changes in settings the jewels — the essentials —would remain the same.

> If the Hindoo wishes to criticize the christian religion he talks of the fables and miracles, and all the nonsense of the Bible, but he does not say one word in disparagement of the sermon on the mount, or of the beautiful life of Jesus. And so when the christian criticizes the Hindoo religion he talks about the dogmas and the temples, but he says nothing [should say nothing] against the morality and philosophy of the Hindoo. Help the Jew and let him help you. Help the Hindoo and let him help you. I deny that any human being has the faculty of seeing good at all who cannot see it in all places. There is the same beauty in the character of Christ and the character of Buddah. It is not an

> assimilation that we want, but adjustment and harmony. I ask the preachers to give up, first, the idea of nationality; and second, the idea of sects. God's children have no sects.
>
> Much has been said about the ladies of India, and of their faults and condition. There are faults; God help us to make them right. We are thankful for your criticism of our women. But while you are speaking of them I will say that I should be glad to see a dozen spiritual women in America. Nice dress, wealth, brilliant society, operas, novels — . Even intellectuality is not all that there is for a man or woman. There should be also spirituality, but that side is entirely absent from christian countries. They live in India.

Vive Kananda's large audience listened very respectfully to his remarks last night, and once or twice applauded heartily.

As The Wave Follows Wave

(*New Discoveries*, Vol. 1, pp. 441-43.)

[*Detroit Tribune*, March 20, 1894]

SO SOUL FOLLOWS SOUL,
ACCORDING TO KANANDA.

Vive Kananda lectured to an audience of about 150 [according to the *Journal*, 500] at the Auditorium last night upon "Buddhism, the Religion of the Light of Asia." (Of which there is no verbatim report available.) Honorable Don M. Dickinson introduced him to the audience.

"Who shall say that this system of religion is divine and that doomed?" asked Mr. Dickinson in his introductory remarks. "Who shall draw the mystic line?"

He also said that at one time the followers of Buddha were the unwilling allies of the christian religion. Kananda appeared in a robe of orange yellow with a sash-like cord about the waist, and a turban draped out of some eastern cloth of silken texture, the flowing end of which was brought in front over one shoulder.

Vive Kananda reviewed at length the early religions of India. He told of the great slaughter of animals on the altar of sacrifice; of Buddha's birth and life; of his puzzling questions to himself over the causes of creation and the reasons for existence; of the earnest struggle of Buddha to find the solution of creation and life; of the final result.

Buddha, he said, stood head and shoulders above all other men. He was one, he said, [of] whom his friends or enemies could never say that he drew a breath or ate a crumb of bread but for the good of all.

"He never preached transmigration of the soul," said Kananda,

> except he believed one soul was to its successor like the wave of the ocean that grew and died away, leaving naught to the succeeding wave but its force. He never preached that there was a God, nor did he deny there was a God.
>
> "Why should we be good?" his disciples asked of him.

> "Because," he said, "you inherited good. Let you in your turn leave some heritage of good to your successors. Let us all help the onward march of accumulated goodness, for goodness' sake."
>
> He was the first prophet. He never abused any one or arrogated anything to himself. He believed in our working out our own salvation in religion.
>
> "I can't tell you," he said, on his death bed, "nor any one. Depend not on any one. Work out your own religion [salvation]."
>
> He protested against the inequality of man and man, or of man and beast. All life was equal, he preached. He was the first man to uphold the doctrine of prohibition in liquors. "Be good and do good," he said. "If there is a God you have him by being good. If there is no God, being good is good. He is to be blamed for all he suffers. He is to be praised for all his good."
>
> He was the first who brought the missionaries into existence. He came as a savior to the downtrodden millions of India. They could not understand his philosophy, but they saw the man and his teachings and they followed him.

In conclusion Kananda said that Buddhism was the foundation of the christian religion; that the catholic church came from Buddhism.

Wayside Stories

(*New Discoveries*, Vol. 1, p. 436.)

[Detroit Evening News, March 21, 1894]

Curiosity, says our Hindoo visitor, is the most conspicuous trait of the American people, but he added that it is the way to knowledge. This has long been the European estimate of the American, or more strictly the Yankee character, and perhaps the Hindoo's comment was an echo of what he had heard the Englishmen in India say of the "Yankee."

A Hindoo Monk

(*New Discoveries*, Vol. 2, pp. 6-7. Cf. "Swami Vivekananda on India", (Complete Works, II: 479-81.)

[Bay City Times Press, March 21, 1894]

He gave an interesting lecture at the Opera House last evening. It is rarely that Bay City people have the opportunity of listening to a lecture similar to the one given last evening by Swami Vive Kananda. The gentleman is a native of India, having been born at Calcutta about 30 years ago. The lower floor of the Opera house was about half filled when the speaker was introduced by Dr. C. T. Newkirk. During his discourse, he scored the people of this country for their worship of the almighty dollar. It is true that there is caste in India. There, a murderer can never reach the top. Here, if he gets a million dollars he is as good as any one. In India, if a man is a criminal once, he is degraded forever. One of the great factors in the Hindoo religion is its tolerance of other religions and beliefs. Missionaries are much more severe on the religions of India than upon that of other Oriental countries, because the Hindoos allow them to be, thus carrying out one of their cardinal beliefs, that of toleration. Kananda is a highly educated and polished gentleman. It is said that he was asked in Detroit if the Hindoos throw their children into the river. Whereupon, he replied that they do not, neither do they burn witches at the stake. The speaker lectures in Saginaw tonight.

Kananda Arrives

(New Discoveries, Vol. 2, p. 11.)

[*Saginaw Evening News, March 21, 1894*]

Swami Vive Kananda, the Hindu Monk, arrived this afternoon from Bay City and is registered at the Vincent. He dresses like a well-to-do American and speaks excellent English. He is slightly above the medium height, is stoutly built and his complexion resembles that of an Indian. In answer to a question by a NEWS representative, he said he learned English from private tutors, and by contact with Europeans, who visited Hindustan. He further stated that his talk tonight would be explanatory of the religion of the Hindoo and to show that they are not heathen but believe in a future state.

The Manners And Customs Of India

(The Vedanta Kesari, *1987 Annual Issue, pp. 445-46 and* New Discoveries, Vol. 2. pp. 37-39.)

[The Lynn Daily Evening Item, (date?)]

NORTH SHORE CLUB

The Meeting, Tuesday Afternoon, Addressed by Suami Vive Kananda, a Learned Monk from India – Description of the Manners and Customs of His Country

(Delivered April 17, 1894, of which there is no verbatim transcript available.)

At the meeting of the North Shore Club, Tuesday afternoon, the audience was a large and brilliant one, representing the highest culture, and including many distinguished guests. Suami Vive Kananda, from India, a learned monk, who speaks English with ease and fluency, gave an intensely interesting description of the manners and customs of his country. Suami Vive Kananda, who wore the yellow robe and turban of his order, began by saying that India is divided into two parts, the northern and the southern. In each the language and customs are so different that the speaker who was from the northern portion on meeting a fellow countryman at the Parliament of Religions from the southern, was obliged to converse with him in English, neither being able to understand the other's native language. Throughout the entire country there are nine languages and 100 dialects spoken.

There is some uniformity of religion, yet each sect is a religion and a law unto itself. Many erroneous descriptions have been written about India, based on imperfect knowledge from which inferences have been drawn that have been most prejudicial. With the Hindoo everything is subservient to religion and he gives up all that is antagonistic to it, his creed being that he is not to enjoy life but to conquer it and gain a supreme mastery over self, which is the highest type of civilization. Caste distinctions which are being obliterated are simply the Aryans and the un-Aryans – the Brahmins and the Sudras. The Brahmin, who is the child of a thousand years' culture, must lead a life of rigid discipline; but the Sudra, who is ignorant, is allowed great latitude.

Woman in the position of mother is accorded universal reverence in India. When a son who has become a monk returns to his home, his father, when greeting him, must kneel and touch his forehead to the earth; but the monk must kneel before his mother. Women in India do not throw their children into the rivers to be devoured by crocodiles. Widows are not burned on the funeral pyre of their husband unless it is a voluntary act of self-immolation.

There is no divorce allowed for the high class; a woman who leaves her husband, even if she be most degraded, holds still an interest in his property. Suami Vive Kananda recited a beautiful passage from the Legend of the Ramayana, one of the grandest poems of India, which showed what the love of a wife for her husband should be. The love of Sita for Rama. He added, "Much is said in these days of the 'survival of the fittest,'" and western nations use it as an argument against India, reasoning that their own wealth, prosperity and power show them to be greater and their religion higher and purer.

But India has seen mighty nations rise and fall whose aim has been only the power of conquest and the glory of this life. India has been repeatedly despoiled, has worn the yoke of the conqueror and borne the burden of oppression with indomitable patience and has shown tolerance to all, because she has possessed the knowledge that her people hold fast to a religion that stands securely on a high spirituality and not on the shifting sand of present enjoyment.

A Lecture On "India And Hinduism"

(*New Discoveries*, Vol. 2, p. 42.)

[New York Daily Tribune, April 25, 1894]

Swami Vivekananda lectured before Mrs. Arthur Smith's conversation circle last evening at the Waldorf on "India and Hinduism." (Of which no verbatim transcript is available.) Miss Sara Humbert, contralto, and Miss Annie Wilson, soprano, sang several selections. The lecturer wore an orange-colored coat and the accompanying yellow turban, which is called a beggar's suit. This is worn when a Buddhist has given up "everything for God and humanity." The theory of reincarnation was discussed. The speaker said that many clergymen who were more aggressive than learned asked: "Why one is unconscious of a former life if such a thing had been?" The reply was that "It would be childish to lay a foundation for consciousness, as man is unconscious of his birth in this life, and also of much that has transpired."

The speaker said that "no such thing" as "a Judgment Day" existed in his religion, and that his god neither punished nor rewarded. If wrong was done in any way, the natural punishment was immediate. The soul, he added, passed from one body to another, until it had become a perfect spirit, able to do without the limitations of a body. . . .

At Smith College, Northampton, Massachusetts

(*New Discoveries*, Vol. 2, pp. 36-37.)

[Smith College Monthly, May 1894]

On Sunday, April 15, Swami Vivekananda, the Hindoo monk whose scholarly exposition of Brahmanism caused such favorable comment at the Congress of Religions, spoke at Vespers. (Of which no verbatim transcript is available.) — We say much of the brotherhood of man and the fatherhood of God, but few understand the meaning of these words. True brotherhood is possible only when the soul draws so near to the All-Father that jealousies and petty claims of superiority must vanish because we are so much above them. We must take care lest we become like the frog of the well in the old Hindoo story, who, having lived for a long time in a small place, at last denied the existence of a larger space.

A Lecture On India And Reincarnation

(New Discoveries, Vol. 2, p. 45.)

[New York Daily Tribune, May 3, 1894]

Swami Virekanmda [*sic*] lectured on "India and Reincarnation" last evening at the home of Miss Mary Phillips, No. 19 West Thirty-eighth-st. (Of which no verbatim transcript is available.) He mentioned among other salient points regarding Hindooism, or Brahminism, that their religion bore no distinctive name; that it was considered that a belief in the truth of all creeds was religion, and that the belief that one certain dogma was the real and only religion was sect. The Karmic law of cause and effect was explained, also the external and internal natures in their close relations to each other. The actions in this world, as governed by a previous life and the change to still another life, were dwelt upon in detail.

. . .

Lecture By Hindoo Monk

(*New Discoveries*, Vol. 2, pp. 65-68.)

Swami Vivekananda Tells About the Religion of High Caste Indians

(Of which no verbatim transcript is available.)

[Lawrence, Massachusetts, *Evening Tribune*, May 16, 1894]

Liberty hall was comfortably filled last evening, on the occasion of the lecture by Swami Vivekananda, the noted Brahmin monk, who was a prominent personality at the world's parliament of religions at Chicago last summer, and who is spending some time in this country, studying its manners and customs. The lecture was under the auspices of the woman's club, and was a novel and interesting occasion. The noted Hindu was pleasantly introduced by the president of the club, Miss Wetherbee, who alluded to the great antiquity of India, its wonderful history and the high intellectual qualities of the Hindu race.

The speaker of the evening was attired in native costume, namely, a bright scarlet robe, confined at the waist by a long scarf of the same color, and wore a picturesque white silk turban wound round his head. At the first glance one saw the swarthy complexion, the dark and dreamy eyes and introspective manner of a high caste Brahmin, whose life is devoted to religion and who is also a celibate. That he is a finely educated person, appeared in his wonderful command of English and his power of argument, while an occasional quotation from Milton and Dickens, showed that he was appreciative of the great English classics.

He first spoke of that striking peculiarity of the social condition of the Hindu's caste, affirming that it is not now as strict an institution as in the past, although even now everything goes by heredity. Mixture of castes, though not absolutely forbidden, entails disadvantage on the children. The Brahmin or high caste person devotes the first part of his life to the study of the Vedas or sacred books and the latter part to meditating on the divinity, being supposed to have overcome the human in himself, and to be only a soul.

The speaker did not hesitate to criticise adversely some western customs, especially some connected with the position of woman. He affirmed that we worship women in the wife, while all women to the Hindu represent the mother element. In America when a woman ceases to be young and beautiful, she has a hard time of it, but in India kings must step aside for an aged woman to pass, so great is the respect in which they are held. He affirmed that some of the most beautiful portions of the Vedas, the Hindu bible, were written by women, but that there was no other bible in this world in which they had any part.

Considerable time was given to refuting the statement, which he characterized as untrue, in regard to the cruelty practised to widows in India, the speaker referring in the course of his remarks to the zenana widows, who have been for some time the objective point of Christian missionaries from other countries. Marriage is an institution very safely guarded and, in addition to the law that a Brahmin must not marry a relative, none are allowed to marry who are known to have such a disease as consumption or any incurable physical ill. The strict rules of caste which prevent a person from drinking from the same glass as another, and other kindred regulations, although [not] part of the religion, were excellent in their result on the physical condition of a country, numbering 285 millions, in the prevention of the spread of contagious diseases. The speaker was horrified, as he might well be, at the promiscuous water drinking seen in railroad trains and stations in this country. The children are, first of all, taught kindness to all living beings and so thoroughly is this training that the smallest child instinctively turns aside from stepping on a worm. A strange thought that among these so called heathen there is no need of the society with the long name which often fails in its mission in Christian lands. The guest of a house, that is, a man who comes to the door and says, "I am hungry," is God's own image to the Hindu and is treated with the utmost kindness and consideration, being fed before the master and mistress of the establishment.

The speaker alluded sadly to the poverty of his country, for, while the upper caste live in comfort, there are millions whose only food is dried flowers, and who are so low in the scale of existence that they have hardly an identity, and are pitiful objects in the plane of existence. He hinted quite forcibly that food and education would be better than the sermons which Christians and Mohammedans had been throwing at them for the last hundred years. Many of the simple and primitive customs of this peculiar people were told with naivete and innocence that was refreshing in this age when words are used to conceal thoughts. He said there was no flirting or coquetting between their young men and maids, and that the latter did not strut forth into public places with all their bravery [finery?] on for the purpose of securing a husband, all of which made the inhabitants of this great and glorious republic wonder if something were not slightly rotten in the state of Denmark. It is well to see both sides of the shield in order to be able to decide with an unprejudiced eye, and many of the listeners went away quite puzzled in mind at hearing some of their pet American customs arraigned by a Hindu and a heathen.

The address was a most interesting one and was listened to with deep attention by all present. At the close many [questions] were presented to the thoughtful monk, who wasted very few words in social flourishes or unmeaning talk. He seemed much interested in Dr. Bowker, the only one in the audience who had ever visited the strange land which was centuries old before this republic was born.

The Brahman Monk

(*New Discoveries*, Vol. 2, pp. 68-71.)

Swami Vivekananda the Guest of the Woman's Club

(Of which no verbatim transcript is available Cf. the
preceding
American newspaper report, "Lecture by Hindoo
monk" of the
Lawrence Evening Tribune (pp. 463-66), for other
highlights of the
same lecture.)

[Lawrence American and Andover Advertiser, May 18, 1894]

HE POINTS OUT THE BETTER
PHASES OF BRAHMANISM.

AND DELIVERS A POINTED
MESSAGE TO CHRISTIANS.

Swami Vivekananda, the Brahman monk addressed a most interested audience Tuesday night in Library Hall under the auspices of the Lawrence Woman's Club.

Miss Wetherbee introduced the speaker and prepared the way for a cordial reception which American courtesy rarely fails to give a distinguished visitor from another nation.

Miss Wetherbee wisely referred to him as a prominent personality at the World's Parliament of Religions, also to the strong impression made by him at the World's fair. . . .

His Iterations

. . . In his own country, in his own class, he addresses all women as mother. The Brahmin is educated thus to think of women as mother and a man may not marry his mother. In that country the mother instinct is developed in woman; in this he thought the wife instinct was cultivated, and the most beautiful thing in his lecture was his tribute to the mother, and not unnoticed was the reference to the kindness of heart of the little Hindoo child which would instinctively cause him to turn aside from his path rather than crush a worm.

The Subject of Marriage

formed a large part of his lecture. Among the high classes, called Aryans, women think of marriage as indecent [?]. A widow is not expected to ever marry again. A man who never marries, is highly praised, and indeed worshipped, but should he marry then in the minutes all would be changed. He who does not marry is looked upon as high-minded, as holy and spiritual.

Among the Aryans no money is paid in marriage [?], and as female children are largely in the majority it is one of most difficult things for a father to marry his daughter, and from the time of her birth he racks his brains to find her a husband.

With the two lower classes the rules in regard to marriage are all different. Widows marry again and wives and husbands if desirous become divorced. When a child is born an astrologer comes and casts a horoscope of the child, he delineates the future character of the boy or girl — it is decided whether he is manly or a devilish child; if devilish — he is married to one next in caste, and thus is obtained a minute chance of bettering the condition of the devilish child.

The matter of marriage is not left to the decision of the child as in that case he might marry because [he was] in love with a good nose or good eyes and so in having his own way would spoil the whole thing. The fact was emphasised that only the higher classes think of a

True Spiritual Life

and of worshiping God instead of thinking of marriage. He spoke of the pitiful condition of the lower classes, their poverty and their ignorance. Millions and millions are [un]able to write their name and yet he said:

> We are all preaching sermons into them, when their hands are reaching out for bread. Poverty is so extreme in the lower classes that fifty cents a month is the average income of a Hindoo. Millions live on one poor meal a day and millions subsist on wild flowers for food.

He spoke of the idea being prevalent that there were no scholars among the women of India and stated that this was an error as many women of the Brahmins were married but became scholars, and with evident pride he referred to the fact that in no nation could one line be found

In Any Bible

that had been written by a woman excepting his own country alone where many beautiful things in their Bible had been written by women.

Swami Vivekananda did not fail to inform the audience in English words which could not be misunderstood, that the effort to raise his people by teaching them the Christian religion was a thankless task. He said:

> We have seen the Greek and the Persian come to us — we have seen the Spaniard with guns come to make us Christians, still we are Hindoos and thus we shall remain.

Had Vivekananda used all the power of his flashing eyes and his expressive voice it would have been a most dramatic speech when he said:

> I dare here in America to say that we of India shall stand by our religion.

He said our customs were good for us and we were welcome to them. He stood before us as he has before many a cultured American audience — he, the learned exponent of the Brahman religion, the only Hindoo who has ever come to this country to tell us — as forcibly as he dared and as politely as he could and yet be forcible, — to say no more to the poor Hindoo but to be so very kind as to mind our own business.

After the lecture many of the audience gladly availed themselves of the opportunity offered by Mr. and Mrs. Young to meet Vivekananda at their residence where he has been entertained and has proven himself to be a most delightful guest.

Swami Vivekananda

(*New Discoveries*, Vol. 2, pp. 144-145.)

[Mrs. Ole Bull submitted to the Boston Evening Transcript the following report of Swami Vivekananda's public lecture at Greenacre, Maine, delivered Friday, August 3, 1894, of which there is no verbatim transcript available. Vide the notes from discourses given at Greenacre, Maine, entitled "The Religion of India", in this volume of the Complete Works.]

[Boston Evening Transcript, August 11, 1894]

A defense of Mahomet [*sic*] by a Hindu to a Christian audience; the lesson that all prophets are to be revered and their teachings studied reverently; that the followers of these teachers should not confound for us by their behavior the revelation made from God to man by prophecy — was the theme at Greenacre yesterday.

Clear thought and statement patiently corrected the crude and superficial adverse criticism and comment that had been made concerning the Eastern belief — reincarnation. The statement was masterful, because simple, and was brought home by illustrations familiar and commonplace. This was followed by a nobly eloquent plea for the judicial spirit in judging the history of the time and the faith of Mahomet himself and the service done the human race by the essentials of this faith as a prophet of God. Men and women present, many of whom fear the heathen, were moved as they tell us Wendell Phillips (American orator and reformer (1811-1884).) was wont to move the hard hearts to consider the sin of slavery.

Scorn, wit and intellect did noble service in all gentleness and dignity in this appeal that the defects, the horrors, of each and all religions should be put one side that the essentials common to all — the immortality of the soul, one God, the Father and his prophets sacred, each, to some division of the human family, and each having truth to give needful to all — should be recognized and reverenced to salvation.

The speaker, Swami Vivekananda, gave what only a great soul is capable of giving. It was an hour never to be forgotten. This man brought those present into the light of truth, whatever their prejudice and training, as Phillips Brooks united Unitarian and Episcopalianism, and all who love the good and true came to hold him for their bishop. So this Hindu, in his constructive thought, when he will give it, can make the power of the prophets known to us by his own presence.

Nirvanashatkam*

(*New Discoveries*, Vol. 2, pp. 149-50
(Arena, October 1899, p. 499).)

[Swami Vivekananda's partial translation of the "Nirvânashatkam" by Shankara, recited at Greenacre, Maine, and reported in an 1894 issue of the Greenacre Voice]

(*Vide* the notes from discourses delivered at Greenacre, Maine, entitled "The Religion of India", in this volume of the *Complete Works* pp. 267-71

Under the Swami's famous pine at Greenacre, Vivekananda said:

"I am neither body nor changes of the body; nor am I senses nor objects of the senses. I am Existence Absolute. Bliss Absolute. Knowledge Absolute. I am It. I am It.

"I am neither death nor fear of death; nor was I ever born, nor had I parents. I am Existence Absolute. Bliss Absolute. Knowledge Absolute. I am It. I am It.

"I am not misery nor have I misery. I am not enemy nor have I enemies. I am Existence Absolute. Bliss Absolute. Knowledge Absolute. I am It. I am It.

"I am without form, without limit, beyond space, beyond time; I am in everything, I am the basis of the universe — everywhere am I. I am Existence Absolute. Bliss Absolute. Knowledge Absolute. I am It. I am It."

The Nonsense Of Nations

(*New Discoveries*, Vol. 2, pp. 154-155.)

[Boston Evening Transcript, August 15, 1894]

A short résumé is given below of the last of the talks of Vivekananda under the pines at Eliot, (Of which no verbatim transcript is available. *Vide* "The Religion of India" — notes from discourses delivered at Greenacre, Maine — in the temple of the gods, to paraphrase Bryant's (William Cullen Bryant (1794–1878).) line —

> "The groves were God's first Temple."
>
> What is the nation? What is law? We have laws only that we may become outlaws (above law).
>
> There is the freedom of the soul; through this we know the freedom of law. I am of the nation of those who seek the liberty of the soul. I am of the nation of those who worship God.
>
> The divine ones of God are all my Masters. I learn of your Christ in learning of Krishna, of Buddha, in learning of Mohamet. I worship God alone. "I am existence absolute, bliss absolute, Knowledge Absolute." I condemn nothing that I find in nation, state or religion, finding God in all. Our growth is not from evil to good, but from good to better, and so on and on. I learn from all that is called evil or good. The nation and all such nonsense may go. It is love, love, love God and my brother.

A High Priest Of India

(*New Discoveries*, Vol. 2, pp. 191-192.)

[*Baltimore American*, October 13, 1894]

SWAMI VIVEKANANDA ARRIVES IN BALTIMORE

HIS VIEWS ON RELIGION

Swami Vivekananda, a Brahmin high priest of India, arrived in Baltimore last night, and is the guest of Rev. Walter Vrooman. . . .

To an American reporter last night Swami Vivekananda said:

> I have been very favorably impressed with American institutions during my stay in this country. My time has been divided between four cities — Chicago, New York, Boston and Detroit. I never heard of Chicago when in India, but I had frequently heard of Baltimore. The main criticism I have to pass on America is that you have too little religion here. In India they have too much. I think the world would be better if some of India's surplus of religion could be sent over here, while it would be to India's profit if its people could have some of America's industrial advancement and civilization. I am a believer in all religions. I think there is truth in my religion; I think there is truth in your religion. It is the same truth in all religions applying itself through various channels to the same end. I think the great need of the world is less law, and more godly men and women. . . .

Priest Swami In Town

(*New Discoveries*, Vol. 2, pp. 196-200.)

[Baltimore News, October 13, 1894]

A High Caste Hindoo Visiting in Baltimore

HIS GORGEOUS GARB ATTRACTS MUCH ATTENTION IN THE LOBBY AT THE RENNERT – HE WHISTLES AND INDULGES IN EAST INDIAN WIT – HE COMES TO BALTIMORE ON A TOUR OF THE COUNTRY AND WILL SPEAK AT THE LYCEUM TOMORROW NIGHT.

Swami Vivekananda, High Priest of the Hindoos, walked into the lobby of the Hotel Rennert this forenoon attired in a flaming red cloak and a gaudy yellow turban that made him the centre of all eyes. . . .

His Idea of Humor

Swami Vivekananda has the sense of humor about him. He was talking this morning about the Food Show, which he intends to visit. He says he doesn't know much about food except to swallow it, and that is a very representative specimen of the wit of Ormus (Hormuz, or Ormuz, an ancient Iranian town.) and of Ind.

Another time he spoke of women's rights and said laughingly that women had more rights the world over than they were credited with having. When he changed his black coat, before going to the Rennert, and put on the cardinal red garment with the yellow turban he came out of his room smiling, and said:

"A transformation!"

The High Priest can whistle and has enough music in his soul to start the tunes in class-meeting if he were Methodist instead of Hindoo. He whistled a couple of strains in his room this morning for a reporter of The News. It was not "Daisy Bell" nor yet "Sweet Marie," and must have been some sort of a heathen Hindoo jingle. . . .

Views on Topics of the Day

Swami is traveling around the country, as he says, lecturing and studying American institutions, but he seems not to have got much into the pith of American sociology, for he knows nothing of such questions as European immigration, divorce, the race problem, etc., which are worrying the economists of the land.

He is, however, posted on Oriental immigration, and says the United States has no right to bar out the Chinese. He says the law of love must prevail and force must yield. He predicts the downfall of any nation that uses force. He says also that the United States should open her doors to the world. He believes the Southern part of the continent should be filled with Hindoos and Chinese.

"There is no such thing as divorce in India," he said;

> our law does not allow it. Our women are more limited in their sphere than the women of America. Some of them are as highly educated. They are entering the medical profession to some extent now. I see no reason why American women should not vote.

He evaded a question as to the position of Hindoo women in their homes and their treatment by their husbands. It may be that he does not know much about it. He is not a married man. Priests of his caste do not marry.

He mentioned two things which he said had impressed him in America. One was the absence of poverty in the country at large, and the other was the unusual prevalence of ignorance in the South.

Likes the Elevator

When he went to the elevator at the Rennert he said:

> There is an American institution which we do not have to any extent in India. I like it very much.

A lady was just coming off the elevator. She was somewhat startled by the red and yellow costume of the priest, but his imperturbable countenance gave no sign of consciousness of the attention he attracted.

His address tomorrow night at the Lyceum will be mainly introductory of himself and explanatory of the Hindoo nation. He will speak briefly, but will remain in Baltimore and speak more at length a week from tomorrow night.

A Wise Man Among Us

(*New Discoveries*, Vol. 2, pp. 200-202.)

[Baltimore Sunday Herald, October 14, 1894]

Visit of a Distinguished Hindoo Priest to This City

HE IS A GUEST OF THE VROOMAN BROTHERS AND IS INTERESTED IN THE ESTABLISHMENT OF AN INTERNATIONAL UNIVERSITY OF RELIGIONS — HIS GORGEOUS GARB.

. . . . . .

. . . Mr. Vivecananda conversed with a *Sunday Herald* reporter, speaking English with ease and with an accent similar to that of an educated Italian. He displayed the greatest familiarity with the institutions of this country, religious, political and social.

Mr. Vivecananda came to Baltimore at the invitation of the Vrooman brothers, Hiram, Carl and Walter, and while in this city will be their guest. Rev. Hiram Vrooman was seen at his residence, 1122 North Calvert Street, yesterday, and talked freely in reference to the visit of the distinguished guest.

"Mr. Vivecananda," he said, "is one of the most intelligent men I have ever met. He came to this city at our invitation, and while here will confer with us in reference to the founding of the international university, which it is proposed to establish as an outcome of the World's Congress of Religions, which was such an interesting feature of the World's Fair. This university is one of Mr. Vivecananda's pet ideas, and has the full sympathy of myself and my brothers, and also a number of gentlemen of wealth and position, including several religions. Among its promoters are members of the Roman Catholic and Hebrew religions. The idea of the university is education in general religion. . . .

"One of Mr. Vivecananda's ideas in the establishing of the university is that it may serve to educate a superior kind of missionary for work in India. While he is steadfast to his own religious belief, he wishes that the present system of sending ignorant men as missionaries to India may be discontinued and men sent there who can teach the Christian religion from an elevated standpoint. In this wish he is animated only by a desire for the good of general religion. . . .

"Mr. Vivecananda told me that his father was a great believer in the Lord Jesus, as he called Him, and that when a boy he had read in the Gospel of St. John the thrilling description of the crucifixion of the Savior and wept over it. He will remain in this city for several weeks. To-morrow evening he will deliver a brief address at our meeting at the Lyceum, and on Sunday week will speak at length at our second meeting on the university plan."

Love Religion's Essence

(Ray and Wanda Ellis, "Swami Vivekananda in Washington D.C.", *The Vedanta Kesari*, 1991, pp. 370-73.)

Vive Kananda, a Brahmin Monk, Preaches at the People's Church

[*Washington Times*, Monday, October 29, 1894]

Vive Kananda, the Brahmin monk, spoke to the congregation of the People's Church, No. 423 G Street northwest, at 11:00 a.m. yesterday. (On Sunday, October 28, 1894, Swami Vivekananda delivered two talks at the People's Church, of which there are no verbatim transcripts available. Cf. Complete Works, II: 497-99 for an interview with the Swami given after this morning sermon.) . . . Dr. Kent introduced the monk. . . .

Vive Kananda, coming forward, said as a boy at the university he studied comparative religion. In India are many religions. One-fifth are Mahomedans. A million are Christians. He studied all. He listened to a great Hindoo preacher, and when he had finished, said:

"My brother, have you seen God?

"The preacher looked up in surprise.

"No."

"How, then, do you know these things are true?"

"My father told me."

"Who told your father?"

"His father," and so on through his ancestors to the clouds.

He heard a Christian preacher of great eloquence. This man told the seeker for truth that if he was not immersed in water at once he was in great danger to be roasted alive. Upon further questions this Christian also, through the records of his books, went back to his ancestors, and so back to the clouds.

The Student Not Satisfied

This did not satisfy the student. He set about praying. He prayed sometimes three days and nights with much weeping and without food. He finally found a man who knew no books, not even to write his own name. This sage was preaching his religion. When asked the old question, he replied:

"Yes, I see God now and I will teach you to see Him."

This man bore the stamp of God in his features. It was the same certificate that came to the man of Nazareth when the dove descended upon Him at Jordan. He made his hearer to believe that God lives and religion is not a mockery.

For twelve years Kananda sat at this man's feet. He was the master. He said one day, "Take up this book." Kananda took up the book and read. It was a calendar. He read in it where the rainfall was foretold. It said that within a certain time so many tons of rain would fall in a certain district. "Now," said the teacher, "close the book and press it." He did so. "Squeeze it very hard." He obeyed. "Did any water come from the book?" "None." So are all books. The true religion is here, at the heart.

The truth is people do not want God. Far from it. Religion is largely fashionable. My lady has a fine parlor, elegant furniture, a piano, beautiful jewelry, well-fitting, costly dresses, a hat that is the latest thing out. She cannot get along without a dash of religion to keep up with her set. There is much of this religion, but it is hypocrisy, and hypocrisy is the root of all evil. This sort of religion is not of God. It is only the shadow. People with such religion sometimes grow to be in earnest and talk about religious things as if they had some reality. So talking about religion without having it these people fall to quarreling and fighting. "Mine, mine," is the cry, never "thine, thine." "My religion is best." "No, mine," and so they fight as did the savage tribes about their rival gods, Mambo and Jumbo. Competition in religion, as in business, is the bane of all.

Love Abideth

Your own Paul says "all else shall perish, but love abideth." That is the great truth. That false doctrine that my nation shall be aggrandized at the cost of every other nation is not of God.

A youth went to his master and said, "I want to know God." The master paid little attention, but the youth persisted and would not be put off. Finally one day the master said: "Let us go down to the river and have a bath." So they went down and the youth plunged in. The master followed and falling upon him held him under. The youth struggled, but the master would not let him up. Finally, when he seemed to be almost dead he desisted, drew him from the water and revived him. "What did you most want when in the water?" the master asked. "Breath," was the answer. "Then you don't want God."

So it is with men, what do you want? You want breath, without it you cannot live; you want bread, without it you cannot live; you want a house, without it you cannot live. When you want God as you want these things, He manifests himself to you. It is a great thing to want God.

A majority of men and women in this world want the enjoyments of sense. They have been told that there is a God afar off and if they will send him a cartload of words he will help them get these good things of this world. But in every land there are a few persons who want God. They would be one with the essence of good and truth. Religion is not shopkeeping. Love asks no return; love begs not; love gives.

Religion is not an outgrowth of fear; religion is joyous. It is the spontaneous outburst of the songs of birds and the beautiful sight of the morning. It is an expression of the spirit. It is from within an expression of the free and noble spirit.

If misery is religion, what is hell? No man has a right to make himself miserable. To do so is a mistake; it is a sin. Every peal of laughter is a prayer sent to God.

To go back, what I have learned is this: Religion is not in books, not in forms, not in sects, not in nations; religion is in the human heart. It is engraved there. The proof of it is in ourselves.

I make two points. There are sects. Let them go on increasing in number till each is a sect by himself. None can see God exactly as another; each must believe in Him and serve Him as he sees Him. Then I want a harmonizing of the sects. Individuality is not in a fight with universality.

Let each for himself and all together fight evils. If you have a power of eight and I a power of four, and you come and destroy me, you have lost at least four. You have only four left to conquer evil. It is love alone that can conquer hatred. If there is power in hate there is infinitely more power in love.

The Hindoo Optimistic

(Ray and Wanda Ellis, "Swami Vivekananda in Washington D.C., *The Vedanta Kesari*, 1991, pp. 369-70.)

[*Washington Times*, November 2, 1894]

Reincarnation

(The untranscribed lecture advertised as "Karma and Reincarnation", delivered at the People's Church, Sunday, October 28, 1894.)

Optimism is the feature of the belief of the Aryas or Hindoos as distinguished from Western religions, according to the Brahman monk, Vive Kananda, who spoke to a fair-sized audience at Metzerott Hall last night. His subject was reincarnation. Much of his lecture was devoted to comparison of Hindoo with Christian doctrine.

To illustrate the tenet of reincarnation he compared the human body to a river. Each drop of water passes on and is replaced by another. The entire body of water, he observed, changes wholly in a few moments, but we call it the same river. In the same way the particles of the body are constantly replaced by others and no two days do we have the same body, yet we preserve our identity.

The spirit remains so, the Hindoos believe, that the person may have a different and more sudden and violent change in death and yet pass on in its existence to some other place in the universe, to some other planet or star, and then take on a body of flesh again or of some other kind.

He said there ought to be no talk of sin. The mistakes of the past ought to be used only for guidance in the future, never to be moaned over. When the lesson is learned from them they should be forgotten.

"Strike a light," he said, "sit not in darkness and sorrow. Do always better and be happy." . . .

Vivekananda's Lecture

(*New Discoveries*, Vol. 2, p. 203.)

[*Baltimore News*, November 3, 1894]

Swami Vivekananda, Hindoo high priest, lectured last night at Harris' Academy of Music Concert Hall. His subject was "India and Its Religion." (Of which no verbatim transcript is available.) He explained the belief of the various Eastern religions, including his own, which is Brahminism. He ridiculed the idea of sending missionaries of so many different faiths to heathen lands, and said that the various religions engaged in missionary work should be united. Mr. Vivekananda explained that the Hindoo religion is optimistic and not pessimistic. His main point was the doctrine of reincarnation, which means that all have existed before and will live again in other forms. The proceeds of the lecture will be applied to the work of founding an international college.

Let India Alone

(*New Discoveries*, Vol. 2, p. 314.)

[*Daily Eagle*, April 8, 1895]

Then It will Come Out All Right, Says Swami Vivekananda

The English people were given a raking over last night by Swami Vivekananda of India, who lectured to a throng at the Pouch mansion. (Of which no verbatim transcript is available. Cf. the newspaper report "Some Customs of the Hindus", Complete Works, II: 515-17, for a complementary report of the same lecture.) He said that the English used three B's — Bible, brandy and bayonets — in civilizing India. The preacher went ahead with the Bible to get the lay of the fortifications. The English, he said, had exaggerated the social conditions of India in their writings. They got their ideas from the Pariahs, who were a sort of human scavenger. No self-respecting Hindoo, he declared, would associate with an Englishman. The story about widows throwing themselves under the chariot of Juggernaut he declared to be a myth. Child marriage and caste he agreed were bad. Caste, he said, originated with the mechanics' guilds. What India needed was to be let alone, and it would come out all right.

Abou Ben Adhem's Ideal

(*New Discoveries*, Vol. 3, pp. 316-18. Abou Ben Adhem, the hero of Leigh Hunt's famous poem, asked a recording angel to list him as loving his fellowmen.)

[*New York World*, December 8, 1895]

SWAMI VIVEKANANDA THE YOGI,
COMES FROM BOMBAY,

PREACHING LOVE FOR HIS FELLOW-MAN.

To find an ascetic of the Highest Eastern type clad in a red and flowing Hindoo cloak over unmistakable American trousers is necessarily a surprise. But in other things besides dress is Swami Vivekananda astonishing. In the first place he declares that your religion or any one else's religion is just as good as his own, and if you should happen to be a Christian or Mussulman, Baptist or Brahmin, atheist, agnostic or Catholic, it will make no difference to him. All that he asks is that you act righteously according to your lights.

The Yogi, with his peculiar notions of dress and worship, arrived Friday on the Brittanic. He went to No. 228 West Thirty—ninth street. While in New York he will lecture upon metaphysics and psychology, and will also disseminate in a general way his ideas on the universal religion which asks no man to take another by the throat because his creed happens to be different. "Let me help my fellowman; that is all I seek," he says.

"There are four general types of men," he says,

> the rational, the emotional, the mystical and the worker. For them we must have their proper worship. There comes the rational man, who says, "I care not for this form of worship. Give me the philosophical, the rational — that I can appreciate." So for the rational man is the rational, philosophic worship.
>
> There comes the worker. He says: "I care not for the worship of the philosopher. Give me work to do for my fellow-men." So for him is made a worship, as for the mystical the emotional. In the religion for all these men are the elements of their faith.

"No," said the Swami, very softly, in answer to a question,

> I do not believe in the occult. If a thing be unreal it is not. What is unreal does not exist. Strange things are natural phenomena. I know them to be matters of science. Then they are not occult to me. I do not believe in occult societies. They do no good, and can never do good.

In fact, the Swami belongs to no society, cult or creed. His is a religion which compasses all worship, all classes, all beliefs.

Swami, who is a very dark-featured and good-looking young fellow, explained his creed yesterday in remarkably pure English. One forgot when he spoke that an orthodox choker peered over the Bombay robe which in turn scantily concealed the American trousers. One saw instead a winning smile and a pair of deep, lustrous black eyes.

Swami believes in reincarnation. He believes that with the purification of the body the soul rises to a higher condition, and as the purification through matter continues the spirit rises, until released from further migration and is joined with the universal spirit.

Such a man as the Jew-baiter [Hermann?] Ahlwardt, who has just arrived in this country, the Swami cannot understand. "You say," he said,

> that he comes here to preach hate against his fellow-men. Is he not of wrong mind? Is he allowed to spread this hate? The doctors should examine his brain to find out the wrong.

The peculiar name of the Yogi signifies, literally, "The bliss of discrimination." He is the first Indian Yogi who ever came to this country. He comes from Bombay.

The Doctrine Of The Swami

(*New Discoveries*, Vol. 3, pp. 340-41.)

[*New York Herald*, January 19, 1896]

The following is a brief sketch of the Swami's fundamental teachings: (A summary of the Swami's teachings taken from what appears to be a written statement.)

> Every man must develop according to his own nature. As every science has its methods so has every religion. Methods of attaining the end of our religion are called Yoga, and the different forms of Yoga that we teach are adapted to the different natures and temperaments of men. We classify them in the following way, under four heads:
>
> (1) Karma Yoga — The manner in which a man realizes his own divinity through works and duty.
>
> (2) Bhakti Yoga — The realization of a divinity through devotion to and love of a personal God.
>
> (3) Rajah Yoga — The realization of divinity through control of mind.
>
> (4) Gnana Yoga — The realization of man's own divinity through knowledge.
>
> These are all different roads leading to the same center — God. Indeed, the varieties of religious belief are an advantage, since all faiths are good, so far as they encourage man to religious life. The more sects there are the more opportunities there are for making successful appeals to the divine instinct in all men.

"Universal Religion"

(*New Discoveries*, Vol. 3, pp. 475-79.)

Vivekananda's Lecture on the Creeds of the World

[*Hartford Daily Times*, February 1, 1896]

A fair house greeted the Hindu monk, Vivekananda, last night. . . . He was introduced by Mr. C. B. Patterson, in some fitting remarks. . . . His subject last night was "The Ideal, or Universal Religion". ("The Ideal of a Universal Religion" was delivered January 31, 1896, of which there is no verbatim transcript available.)

Throughout the universe there are two forces constantly at work, the centrifugal and centripetal, positive and negative, action and reaction, attraction and repulsion. We find love and hatred, good and evil. What plane is stronger than the spiritual plane, the plane of religion? The world furnishes no hate stronger than that engendered by religion, and no love stronger. No teachings have brought more unhappiness into the world, nor more happiness. The beautiful teachings of Buddha have been carried across the Himalayas, at a height of 20,000 feet, by his disciples. Five hundred years later came the teachings of your beautiful Christ, and these have been carried on the wings of the wind. On the other hand, look at your beautiful earth deluged in blood in the interest of propagandism and religion. As soon as a man comes into the company of those who do not believe as he does, his very nature changes. It is his own opinions he fights for, not religion. He becomes the very embodiment of cruelty and fanaticism. His religion is all right, but when he starts out to fight for his own selfish opinions he is all wrong. People are up in arms about the Armenian and the Turkish butcheries, but their consciences don't say a word when the butcheries are committed in the interest of their own religion. In human beings we find a curious mixture of God, man, and devil, and religion stirs up the latter more than anything else. When we all think alike, the God side of our nature comes out; but let there be a clash of opinions, and presto, change! the devil has the floor. This has been so from time immemorial, and will be so always. In India we know what fanaticism means, for that country for the last thousand years has been the especial field of missionaries. But above the clash of opinions, and the fight for religions, there comes the voice of peace. For 3,000 years efforts have been made to bring the different religions into harmony. But we know how this effort has failed. And it always will fail, and it ought to fail. We have a network of words about love, peace, and universal brotherhood, which were meant all right originally, but we repeat them like parrots, and to us they mean nothing. Is there a universal philosophy for the world? Not yet. Each religion has its own creeds and dogmas and insists upon propagating them. You can't make one religion for the whole world. That must not be. The Armenians say it will be all right if you will all become Armenians. And the Pope of Rome says: "O yea, it is a very easy thing. If you will all become Roman Catholics, it will be all right." And so with the Greek church, and the Protestant church, and all the rest. There can never be one religion only, it would be death to all other religions. If every one thought alike there would be no more thought to think. If everybody looked alike, what monotony! Look alike and think alike — what could we do but sit down and die in despair? We can't live like a row of chipmunks; variation belongs to human life. One God, one religion is an old sing—song, but there's danger in it. But, thank God, it can never be. Start out with your long purse, and your guns and cannon, to push your propagandism. And suppose you succeed for a while? In ten years your so—called unity would be split into fragments. That is why there are so many sects. Take the largest religion, the Buddhist. They try to help the world to be better. Next come the Christians, with [a] good many things to teach. They have three Gods in one, and one in three, and one of the three took on the sins of the world and was killed. Whoever doesn't believe in him, goes to a very hot place. And Mohammed, whoever doesn't believe in him will have his skin burnt off, and then a fresh one will be furnished to be burnt, that he may know that Allah is the all-powerful. All religions came originally from the Orient. These great teachers or incarnations come in different forms. The Hindus have ten incarnations; the first was a fish, and so on, down to the fifth, and from there, they were all men. The Buddhists say: "We don't care to have so many incarnations; we want only one." The Christians say: "We will have only one, and this is Christ." And they say he is the only one. But the Buddhist says they have the start in time; their great teacher came five hundred years earlier. And the Mohammedans say theirs came last, and therefore is the best. Each one loves his own, just as a mother loves her own child. The Buddhist never sees any fault in Buddha; the Christian never sees any fault in Christ, and the Mohammedan never sees any fault in Mohammed. The Christian says their God took the form of a dove and came down, and that they say is not mythology, but history. The Hindu says his god is manifested in a cow and that he says is not superstition, but history. The Jew thinks his Holy of Holies can be contained in a box or chest, with an angel on guard on either side. But the Christian's

God in the form of a beautiful man or woman, is a horrible idol. "Break it down!" they say. One man's prophet did such and such wonderful things, while others call it only superstition. So where's your unity? Then there are your rituals. The Roman Catholic puts on his robe, as I have mine. He has his bells and candles and holy water, and says these are good and necessary, but what you do, he says is only superstition. We can never upset all this and have but one religion for the very life of thought is the differentiation of thought. We must learn to love those who think exactly opposite to us. We have humanity for the background, but each must have his own individuality and his own thought. Push the sects forward and forward till each man and woman are sects unto themselves. We must learn to love the man who differs from us in opinion. We must learn that differentiation is the life of thought. We have one common goal, and that is the perfection of the human soul, the god within us. Religion is the great force to help unfold the god within man. But we have to unfold in our own way. We can't all assimilate the same kind of food. Let your aspirations be of the highest, and your inspirations will be in harmony with reason and all known laws, and the Lord will always be with you.

Vivekananda's Philosophy

(New Discoveries, Vol. 4, p. 20.)

[*Tribune*, March 5, 1896]

He Would Have Many Kinds of Religion

Vivekananda, the Hindoo missionary, lectured at the Hotel Richelieu last night. The parlors of the private hotel were filled to overflowing with a crowd of ladies. When Vivekananda arrived at the hotel it was with difficulty he worked his way in. He went upstairs and very shortly came down again robed in a purple gown, caught about the waist with a purple cord.

Vivekananda in his talk said that there were various religions and each believer thought his religion the only true religion. It was a mistake, he said, to suppose that all should have the same religion.

"If all were of the same religious opinion," said he,

> there would be no religion. No sooner does a religion start than it breaks into pieces. The process is for the religion to go on dividing until each man has his own religion, until each man has thought out his own thoughts and carved out for himself his own religion.

Vivekananda will remain in Detroit about two weeks and will give classes every morning at 11 o'clock and every evening at 8 o'clock at the hotel. . . .

Heard Swami Talk

(New Discoveries, Vol. 4, p. 41.)

[*News Tribune*, March 16, 1896]

VIVEKANANDA LECTURED IN TEMPLE BETH EL

Spoke on the Ideal of a Universal Religion

He Will Probably Leave Tuesday

Temple Beth El was crowded to the doors last night when Swami Vivekananda delivered his address upon "The Ideal of a universal religion." (Of which no verbatim transcript is available.) The time announced for the service was 8 o'clock, but the congregation began to assemble at the temple early in the evening so that the doors had to be opened at 6:25 p.m. They were closed at 7 o'clock and the hundreds that arrived after that time had to be turned away.

> We all hear about universal brotherhood, and how societies stand up and want to preach this. But to what does it amount? As soon as you make a sect you protest against equality, and thus it is no more,

said Swami.

> Unity in variety is the plan of the universe. Just as we are all men, yet we are all separate. We find then, that if by the idea of a universal religion is meant one set of doctrines should be believed by all mankind, it is impossible, it can never be, any more than there will be a time when all faces will be the same. We must not seek that all of us should think alike, like Egyptian mummies in a museum, looking at each other without thought to think. It is this difference of thought, this differentiation, losing of the balance of thought, which is the very soul of our progress, the soul of thought.

Swami will probably leave Tuesday [March 17]. At the close of his address last night he thanked the people of Detroit for the kind reception tendered him and his philosophy.

Philosophy Of Freedom

(*New Discoveries*, Vol. 4, pp. 56-58.)

[*Boston Evening Transcript*, March 21, 1896]

SWAMI VIVEKANANDA COMPARES TEACHINGS OF HINDU WISDOM AND WESTERN RELIGIONS

The Swami Vivekananda, who will be remembered as the Hindu delegate to the World's Parliament of Religions, is in the city as the March class lecturer at the Procopeia, 45 St. Botolph street. (There are no verbatim transcripts available of these classes.) The Swami has been doing some most valuable and successful work in systematic class lecturing in New York, with constantly increasing audiences, during the past two winters, and comes to Boston at a most opportune time.

The Swami gives the following description of his work. In explanation of the term sannyasin, he said, [*Vide* "The Sannyasin", Complete Works, V: 260].

In giving some idea of his work and its methods, the Swami says he left the world because he had a deep interest in religion and philosophy from his childhood, and Indian books teach renunciation as the highest ideal to which a man can aspire.

The Swami['s] teaching, as he expresses it,

> is my own interpretation of our ancient books in the light which my master (a celebrated Hindu sage) shed upon them. I claim no supernatural authority. Whatever in my teachings may appeal to the highest intelligence and be accepted by thinking men, the adoption of that will be my reward. All religions have for their object the teaching of devotion, or knowledge, or activity, in a concrete form. Now, the philosophy of Vedanta is the abstract science which embraces all these methods, and this is what I teach, leaving each one to apply it to his own concrete form. I refer each individual to his own experience, and where reference is made to books, the latter are procurable, and may be studied for each one by himself.

The Swami teaches no authority from hidden beings, through visible objects, any more than he claims learning from hidden books or MSS. He believes no good can come from secret societies.

> Truth stands on its own authority, and truth can bear the
> light of day.

He teaches only the Self, hidden in the heart of every individual, and common to all. A handful of strong men, knowing that Self, and living in its light, would revolutionize the world, even today, as has been the case of single strong men before, each in his day.

His attitude towards Western religions is briefly this. He propounds a philosophy which can serve as a basis to every possible religious system in the world, and his attitude towards all of them is one of extreme sympathy. His teaching is antagonistic to none. He directs his attention to the individual, to make him strong, to teach him that he himself is divine, and he calls upon men to make themselves conscious of divinity within. His hope is to imbue individuals with the teachings to which he has referred, and to encourage them to express these to others in their own way; let them modify them as they will; he does not teach them as dogmas; truth, at length, must inevitably prevail. . . .

Out Of The East

(*New Discoveries*, Vol. 4, pp. 60-62.)

[*Boston Daily Globe*, March 24, 1896]

Message Brought by the Swami Vivekananda — in His Country the Gods Are "Bright Ones" That Help

The Swami Vivekananda is enjoying as great a degree of popularity on his present visit to Boston as he did when society, fashionable, intellectual and faddist, went wild over him on his former visit. . . .

. . . A New York paper published an interview with the Swami, in which he is reported to have expressed the opinion that in Boston "the women are all faddists, all fickle, merely bent on following something new and strange." (Cf. Complete Works, V: 413.) But Swami Vivekananda says that this is an exaggerated and distorted presentation of a criticism which he made upon all American women, that they were too superficial and too prone to follow the sensational and to change from one thing to another. This he says his observation has forced upon him. The American women are intellectual, but they are not steady, serious and sincere.

The first of the Swami's lectures was delivered before an audience of 400 people in the Allen gymnasium, Saturday evening on "The Science of Work," and the second one of the course on "Devotion" was given in the same place, the hall being filled and a number turned away unable to gain admittance.

The lecture was exceedingly interesting and the speaker's manner was very magnetic. In his country, said the Swami, the gods were the "bright ones" who gave help to men and received help from them. The gods are only human beings who are somewhat elevated after death, but God, the highest, is never prayed to or asked for help. He is given only love and worship without anything being asked in return. There are two phases of this God, the one, the abstract God behind the substance of the universe, and the other the personal God who is seen through human intellect and given attributes by it.

The love which is given to God never takes, but always gives, and it does not depend on anything. The worshiper does not pray for health, money or any other thing, but is content with the lot apportioned to him.

People who ask about religion from mere motives of curiosity become faddists, they are always looking for some—thing new and their brains degenerate until they become old rags. It is a religious dissipation with them.

It is not the place that makes heaven or hell, but the mind. Love knows no fear, there can be no love where it is. In love of any sort external objects are only suggested by something within — it is one's own ideal projected, and God is the highest ideal that can be conceived of.

Hatred of the world does not drive good men from it, but the world slips away from the great and saintly. The world, the family and social life, are all training grounds, that is all.

When one realizes that God is love, it does not matter what his other attributes are, that is the only essential.

The more a man throws himself away, the more God comes in, hence self-abnegation, which is the secret of all religion and morality.

Too many people bring down their ideals. They want a comfortable religion, but there is none such. It is all self-surrender and upward striving.

Said A Universal Religion Is Impossible

(*New Discoveries*, Vol. 4, pp.64-65.)

[*Boston Evening Transcript*, March 27, 1896]

Swami Vivekananda told the large audience that crowded the Allen Gymnasium to hear him speak on the "Ideal of a Universal Religion," last night, (Of which no verbatim transcript is available.) that the recent Parliament of Religions at Chicago proved, to that date, that universal religion was impossible. "Nature," he said,

> is wiser than we have thought her to be. It is competition of ideas, the clash of thought, that keeps thought alive. Sects have always been antithetical, and always will be splitting into little varieties of themselves. And the way to get out of this fight of religions is to let the sects go on subdividing.
>
> There is no unity in the three elements of religion — philosophy [theology?], mythology and ceremony. Each theologian wants unity, but his idea of unity is the adjustment of all other creeds to his own. I agree with the old prophets as long as they agree with me. But there is an element of religion that towers above all; that is, philosophy. The philosopher seeks truth, which is one and the same always. And it is acceptable to the four sides of every religious nature — the emotional, mystical, active and philosophical. And he who dares to seek the truth for truth's sake is greatest among men.

For Universal Religion

(*New Discoveries*, Vol. 4, pp. 81-86.)

[*Boston Evening Transcript*, March 30, 1896]

THE HINDU SWAMI LECTURES
BEFORE SEVERAL SOCIETIES.

The Swami Vivekananda has, during the past few days, conducted a most successful work in connection with the Procopeia. During this time he has given four class lectures for the club itself, with constant audiences of between four and five hundred people, at the Allen Gymnasium, 44, St. Botolph street, two at the house of Mrs. Ole Bull in Cambridge, and one before the professors and graduate students of the philosophical department of Harvard University.

The idea, which brought the Swami to America three years ago as Hindu delegate to the Parliament of Religions, and has been the guiding motive of all his subsequent work, both in America and England, is one which appeals strongly to the people whose creation the parliament was, but the methods which he proposes are peculiarly his own. One of his lectures during the week has been "The Ideal of a Universal Religion," (Though this was one of Swami Vivekananda's recurring subjects, there is no available verbatim transcript of this March 26, 1896 lecture. Cf. Complete Works, II: 375-96.) but a "harmonious religion" would, perhaps, equally meet the case, if, indeed, it would not more adequately express that for which he is striving. The Swami is not a preacher of theory. If there is any one feature of the Vedanta philosophy, which he propounds, which appears especially refreshing, it is its intense capability of practical demonstration. We have become almost wedded to the idea that religion is a sublime theory which can be brought into practice and made tangible for us only in another life, but the Swami shows us the folly of this. In preaching the Divinity of Man he inculcates a spirit of strength into us which will have none of those barriers between this life and actual realization of the sublime that, to the ordinary man, appear as insurmountable.

In discussing the general lines on which it appears to him universal religion can alone be established, he claims for his plan no super-authority. As he says:

I have also my little plan. I do not know whether it will work or not, and I want to present it to you for discussion. In the first place, I would ask mankind to recognize this maxim: "Do not destroy." Iconoclastic reformers do no good to the world. Help, if you can; if you cannot, fold your hands, stand by, and see things go on. Therefore say not a word against any man's convictions, so far as they are sincere. Secondly, take man where he stands, and from thence give him a lift. (Cf. Complete Works, II: 384.)

Unity in variety is the plan of the universe. Just as we are all men, yet we are all separate. As humanity, I am one with you; as Mr. So-and-so, I am different from you. As a man you are separate from woman, but as human beings you are all one; as a living being you are one with animals and all that lives, but as man you are separate. That existence is God, the ultimate unity in this universe. In Him we are all one. We find, then, that if by the idea of a universal religion is meant that one set of doctrines should be believed by all mankind, it is impossible, it can never be, any more than all faces will be the same. Again, if we expect that there will be one universal mythology, that is also impossible; it cannot be. Neither can there be a universal ritual. When this time comes the world will be destroyed, because variety is the first principle of life. What makes us formed beings? Differentiation. Perfect balance will be destruction. (Cf. Complete Works, II: 381-82.)

What then do I mean by the ideal of a universal religion? I do not mean a universal philosophy, or a universal mythology, or a universal ritual, but I mean that this world must go on, wheel within wheel. What can we do? We can make it run smoothly, we can lessen friction, we can grease the wheels, as it were. By what? By recognizing variation. Just as we have recognized unity, by our very nature so we must also recognize variation. We must learn that truth may be expressed in a thousand ways, and each one yet be true. We must learn that the same thing can be viewed from a hundred different standpoints, and yet be the same thing. (Cf. Complete Works, II: 382-83.)

In society we see so many various natures of mankind. A practical generalization will be impossible, but for my purpose I have simply characterized them into

> four. First, the active man; then the emotional man; then the mystical man, and lastly the philosopher.
>
> To be universal, religion must provide possibility of realizing truth through means suitable to any one of these minds, and a religion which says that through one alone all men must struggle, whether these minds are capable of the struggle or not, must end in agnosticism.

In his lecture on Karma Yoga, Swami dealt with the science of work. The lecture for the most part analyzed the motives men have in work, and particularly the motive of heaven as a reward for good work on earth. This, said the Swami, is shopkeeping religion. Work alone reaches its highest when it is done absolutely without hope of reward, work for work's sake, and without regard to the consequences.

In discussing Bhakti Yoga, Devotion, the Swami explained the rationale of a Personal God. This idea of devotion and worship of some being who has to be loved, and who can reflect back the love to man, is universal. The lowest stage of the manifestation of this love and devotion is ritualism, when man wants things that are concrete, and abstract ideas are almost impossible. Throughout the history of the world we find man is trying to grasp the abstract through thought forms, or symbols, and the external manifestations of religion. Bells, music, rituals, books, images come under that head. Man can only think with form and word. Immediately thought comes, form and name flash into the mind with them, so that when we think of God, whether as the Personal God with human shape, or as the Divine Principle, or in any other aspect, we are always thinking of our own highest ideal with some or other form, generally human, because the form of man is the highest of which man can conceive. But, while recognizing this as a necessity of human weakness, and while making proportionate use of rituals, symbols, books and churches, we must always remember that it is very good to be born in a church, but it is very bad to die in a church. If a man dies within the bounds of these forms, it shows that he has not grown, that there has been no uncovering of the real, the Divinity, within him.

True love can be regarded as a triangle. The first angle is, love knows no bargain. So when a man is praying to God, "give me this, and give me that," it is not love. How can it be? "I give you my little prayer, and you give me something in return"; that is mere shopkeeping. The second angle is, love knows no fear. So long as God is regarded as a rewarder or a punisher there can be no love for him. The third angle, the apex, is, love is always the highest ideal. When we have reached the point where we can worship the ideal as the ideal, all arguments and doubts have vanished forever. The ideal can never escape, because it is part of our own nature.

In his lecture at Harvard University, (Cf. "The Vedanta Philosophy", Complete Works, I: 357-65, in which there may be some omissions.) the Swami traced the history, so far as is known, of the Vedanta philosophy, and showed to what extent the Vedas (the Hindu scriptures) are accepted as authoritative; merely as the foundation for the philosophy in so far as they appeal to the reason. He compared the three schools, the Dualists, who acknowledge a supreme being, and a lesser being manifesting in men, but eternally separate from men. Next he described the philosophy of the Qualified nondualists, whose particular idea is that there is a God and there is nature, but that the soul and nature is simply the expansion, or the body of God, just as the body of man is to man's soul. They claim, in support of this theory, that the effect is never different from the cause, but that it is the cause reproduced in another form, and as God, therefore, is the cause of this universe, he is also the effect. The Monists . . . declare that if there is a God, that God must be both the material and the efficient cause of the universe. Not only is he the Creator; but he is also the created. He himself is this universe, apparently; but, in reality, this universe does not exist — it is mere hypnotisation. Differentiation is in name and form only. There is but one soul in the universe, not two, because that which is immaterial cannot be bounded, must be infinite; and there cannot be two infinities, because one would limit the other. The soul is pure, and the appearance of evil is just as a piece of crystal, which is pure in itself, but appears to be variously colored when flowers are placed before it.

In discussing Raja Yoga, the psychological way to union with God, the Swami expanded upon the power to which the mind can attain through concentration, both in reference to the physical and the spiritual world. It is the one method that we have in all knowledge. From the lowest to the highest, from the smallest worm to the highest sage, they have to use this one method. The astronomer uses it in order to discover the mysteries of the skies, the chemist in his laboratory, the professor in his chair. This is the one call, the one knock, which opens the gates of nature and lets out the floods of light. This is the one key, the only power — concentration. In the present state of our bodies we are so much distracted, the mind is frittering away its energies upon a hundred sorts of things. By scientific control of the forces which work the body this can be done, and its ultimate effect is realization. Religion cannot consist of talk. It only becomes religion when it becomes tangible, and until we strive to feel that of which we talk so much, we are no better than agnostics, for the latter are sincere and we are not.

The Twentieth Century Club had the Swami as their guest Saturday [March 28], and heard an address from him on the "Practical Side of the Vedanta Philosophy." (Vide Complete Works, I: 387-92 and V: 310-11, respectively, for the lecture and the discussion that followed.) *He leaves Boston today, and will, within a few days, sail for England, en route for India.*

Swami Vivekananda

(*New Discoveries*, Vol. 5, pp. 184-86.)

Lectures on Hindoo Religion and Philosophy

[*Los Angeles Times*, December 9, 1899]

. . . . . .

. . . The well-known expositor of the Hindoo philosophy, dressed in the yellow robe of the Brahmin caste, spoke in part as follows:

> I come before you, ladies and gentlemen, to bring no new religion. I desire simply to tell you a few points that bind together all religions. I shall touch upon some things in the thought of eastern civilization that will appear strange to you and on others that I hope will appeal to you. All the religions of the world have a backbone of unity. This is the principle of philosophy and of toleration.
>
> Very few people in this country understand what India is. It is a country half as large as the United States and containing 300,000,000 people, speaking a number of different tongues, but all bound together by the ideas of a common religion. By these ideas the Hindoos have made their influence felt through the ages, working gently, silently, patiently, while western civilization has been conquering by force of arms. The future will show which is the more powerful — physical force or the power of ideas. The arts and sciences of the Hindoos have found their way over all the earth — their numerals, their mathematical thought, their ethics. Was it not in India, there and there alone, that the doctrine of love was first preached, and not alone the doctrine of love of one's fellow-men, but of love of every living thing, yea, even of the meanest worm that crawls under our feet. When you begin to study the arts and institutions of India, you become magnetized, fascinated. You cannot get away.

In India, as elsewhere, we find the earliest condition one of division into little tribes. These different tribes had each its different god, its different ceremonial. But in coming in contact with one another, the tribes did not follow the course that western civilization has taken — they did not persecute each other because of these differences, but endeavored to find the germs of common ideas in all the religions. And from this endeavor arose the habit of toleration which is the keynote of the Indian religion. Truth is one, can be but one, though it may be expressed in different language.

Another great difference between eastern and western religion lies in the reception of a philosophical and scientific view of the universe. In the West, agnosticism has been growing in late years, and with the loss of a hope in individual immortality, which the westerner is always desiring and seeking, a note of despair has crept into western thought. Ages ago, the Hindoo realized that the universe was one of law, and that, under law, all change. Therefore, an imperishable individuality is an impossibility. But this thought is not one of despair to the Hindoo. On the contrary — and this is what the westerner can least understand of eastern thought — he longs for freedom, for release from the thralldom of the senses, from the thralldom of pain and the thralldom of pleasure.

Western civilization has sought a personal God and despaired at the loss of belief in such. The Hindoo, too, has sought. But God cannot be known to the external senses. The Infinite, the Absolute, cannot be grasped. Yet although it eludes us, we may not infer its non-existence. It exists. What is it that cannot be seen by the outward eye? The eye itself. It may behold all other things, but itself it cannot mirror. This, then, is the solution. If God may not be found by the outer senses, turn your eye inward and find, in yourself, the soul of all souls. Man himself is the All. I cannot know the fundamental reality, because I am that fundamental reality. There is no duality. This is the solution of all questions of metaphysics and ethics. Western civilization has in vain endeavored to find a reason for altruism. Here it is. I am my brother, and his pain is mine. I cannot injure him without injuring myself, or do ill to other beings without bringing that ill upon my own soul. When I have realized that I myself am the Absolute, for me there is no more death nor life nor pain nor pleasure, nor caste nor sex. How can that which is absolute die or be born? The pages of nature are turned before us like the pages of a book, and we think that we ourselves are turning, while in reality we remain ever the same.

Hindu Philosophy

(*New Discoveries*, Vol. 5, pp. 194-95.)

Conception Of The Universe In Distant India

[*Los Angeles Times*, December 13, 1899]

Swami Vivekananda, the Hindu philosopher, addressed the regular monthly meeting of the Southern California Academy of Sciences at Unity Church last evening. (Cf. the following December 13, 1899 Los Angeles Herald newspaper report on the same lecture (pp. 502-4).) The audience was large and appreciative, and at the end of the lecture a number of questions were asked by members of the audience and answered by the lecturer. . . .

The speaker began with a reference to the mythological tales of the Hindus in which they attempted to explain the origin of the universe, and he told also of the endeavors of the ancients to explain the mysteries which surrounded them.

According to their belief, he said, man's first idea is of himself. His will moves all his members. A child's idea of power is in its will. All movement of the universe has a will behind it. The Hindus believe, said the speaker, that there is but one God, and he a person like the rest of them, but infinitely greater. Their mind is philosophical enough not to admit the existence of two gods, one bad and one good. With them nature is a unit, unity in all existence is the universe, and God is the same as nature.

"There is not a system of philosophy," said the speaker,

> from that of the ancient Egyptians down to that of the Roman Catholic Church, which does not show traces of the same thought. All forces that exist in the mental and physical world have been resolved, in India, into the one word "Father" ["Prâna"?]. Whatever is, has been projected by Him.

In closing, the philosopher said that the ancient voice of India had found an echo in the 19th century in the writings of Herbert Spencer.

Conception Of The Universe

(*New Discoveries*, Vol. 5, pp. 192-94.)

[*Los Angeles Herald*, December 13, 1899]

Swami Vivekananda's lecture before the Academy of Sciences

Unity church was filled last evening with a large audience to hear the Swami Vivekananda, a native of India, lecture on the kosmos, or the Veda conception of the universe (This was Swami Vivekananda's second lecture in California, entitled "The Cosmos, or the Veda Conception of the Universe", of which there is no verbatim transcript available. Cf. the Swami's two New York lectures on the Cosmos delivered in 1896 in Complete Works, II ("The Cosmos: The Macrocosm" and "The Cosmos: The Microcosm").) under the auspices of the Southern California Academy of Sciences. . . .

In introducing his subject the speaker reviewed the mythology of the flood, which among the Babylonians, Egyptians, Assyrians and other races is similar to the story of the Hebrew scriptures, showing that all held a similar belief concerning the creation of the universe.

> In the worship of the sun and the forces of nature, we see the attempts of ancient peoples to explain the mysteries surrounding them. Man's first idea of force was himself. When a stone fell he saw no force in it but the will behind it, and he conceived the idea that the whole universe was moved by force of wills. Gradually these wills became one, and science begins to rise. Gods begin to vanish, and in their place comes oneness, and now God is in danger of being dethroned by modern science. Science wants to explain things by their own nature and make the universe self-sufficient.
>
> Wills gradually began to disappear, and in their place comes will. This was the process of development in all the nations of the world, and so it was in India. Their ideas and gods were pretty much the same as those of other lands, only in India they did not stop there. They learned that life alone can produce life, and that death can never produce life. In our speculations about God we have got to monotheism.

Everywhere else speculation stops there; we make it the be all and end all of everything, but in India it does not stop there. A gigantic will can not explain all this phenomena we see around us. Even in man there is something back of the will. In so common sense a thing as the circulation of the blood, we find will is not the motive power.

We have conceived God as a person like ourselves, only infinitely greater, and because there is goodness and mercy and happiness in the world there must be a being possessing these attributes, but there is also evil. The Hindu mind is too philosophical to admit the existence of two gods, one good and one bad. India remained true to the idea of unity. What is evil to me may be good to someone else; what is good to me may be evil to others. We are all links in a chain. Hence comes the speculation of the Upanishads, the religion of 300,000,000 of the human race. Nature is a unit; unity is in all existence, and God is the same as nature. This is one of the Indian speculations known to all the world outside of India.

There is not a system of religion or philosophy in the world that does not show the influence of India's speculation, even to the Catholic church. The conservation of energy, considered a new discovery, has been known there by the name of father [Prâna?]. Whatever is comes from the father. Brahma [Prana?] must energize on something, and that they say is an invisible ether. Brahma [Prana?] vibrating on ether, the solid, the liquid, the luminous, it is all the same ether. The potentiality of everything is there. In the beginning of the next period Brahma [Prana?] will begin to vibrate more and more.

Thus this speculation of India's scriptures is very similar to modern science. The same idea is taken up by modern evolution. Even our bodies, different only in dignity, are links in the same chain. In one individual the possibilities of every other individual are there. The living entity contains the possibility of all life, but can only express that which environment demands. The most wonderful speculations are formed in modern science. The one that interests me as a preacher of religion is the oneness of all religions [life?]. When Herbert Spencer's voice says that the same life welling up in the plant is the life welling up in the individual, the Indian religion has found a voice in the nineteenth century.

Told About India

(*New Discoveries*, Vol. 5, pp. 227-29.)

[*Los Angeles Herald*, January 3, 1900]

Lecture last night at Blanchard Hall by Swami Vivekananda

Swami Vivekananda, member of an ancient order of Hindu monks, who is giving a series of lessons and lectures in this city, addressed an audience last night at Blanchard hall upon the "History of India" ["The People of India"]. (Of which no verbatim transcript is available.) The Swami appeared before his audience in American dress, losing to a great degree the peculiar and characteristic personality given him by the aesthetic silken robes and the turban worn by his order.

The speaker said India was not a country, but a continent containing a huge mass of races united by religion. India was of ancient date. It was inhabited, when through a desire to reach it by a shorter passage, Columbus discovered America, and its production of cotton, sugar, indigo and spices have enriched the world. This country inhabited by 200,000,000 of people, is full of little villages that extend through all the valleys and up the mountains thousands of feet above the sea level. The immense fertility of the soil owes much to the tremendous rainfall, which is often 1,800 inches [*sic*] in a season, averaging perhaps 600 inches. Many of the people, however, in spite of the abundant productions, live wholly on millet, a kind of cereal; no animal food is eaten; no meat, eggs or fish.

The country from most ancient times has kept its own customs, its own languages and its castes. It has by its religion saved itself while it has seen other sections [nations] rise and decay. The Babylonian civilization was not new, but India dates long before its rise and fall. The most ancient language, Sanskrit, is spoken by the priests, and was spoken once by all the different races. The speaker gave examples of many of our common English words coming from Sanskrit roots, and traced the old religious ideas and even mythology to the ancient Aryan races.

Many of the customs of the country were sketched, and further it was shown how this country was the seat of civilization, the center of arts, the sciences, the philosophical thought of the world.

The people of India have saved themselves by making a wall around themselves by making the castes absolute. An emperor in India is glad to trace his descent from a priest, who is the highest caste. The castes do not exist as they did once, but they are divided into many divisions and sub-divisions. There are hundreds of them. No people of different castes eat together, or cook together. Marriage is not legal if made outside of one's caste. The intricacy of the laws of caste is very great and branch out into the minutest detail. The poorest beggar or the viceroy of India may belong to the same caste.

Shoes are not allowed to be worn, as they are made from the skin of an animal. The women pay even more attention to these details than the men. All these customs have their philosophy. This is the true democracy, it is the socialistic idea, the development of the masses, not the individual.

The speaker closed with comparing the position of women in India with that of this country. In India the whole idea of womanhood is the mother. The mother is reverenced. She is the giver of life, the founder of the race.

The Religious Legends Of India*

(*New Discoveries*, Vol. 5, p. 269.)

[*Los Angeles Times*, January 17, 1900]

The Swami

Clad in his maroon robe, Swami Vivekananda addressed a small audience composed mostly of women, at the Shakespeare Club this evening [January 16]. (Of which no verbatim transcript is available.) He gave an account of the religious legends of Brahmanism, which are embodied in the daily lives of the Hindus, of the origin of Shiva and his surrender to the pure spirit of his wife, today the mother of all India, whose worship is carried to such an extent that no female animal can be killed. Vivekananda quoted freely from the Sanskrit, translating as he went along. . . .

The Science Of Yoga

(*New Discoveries,* Vol. 5, p. 276.)

[*Los Angeles Herald,* January 26, 1900]

Swami Vivekananda, the Oriental seer, lectured at the Shakespeare club this morning [Thursday, January 25] on "The Science of Yoga". (Of which no verbatim transcript is available.) He said that there is no difference in kind between anything in nature, but that all differences are of degree merely. The mind is the supreme power, the motor of the world.

Swami Vivekananda At The Los Angeles Home

(*New Discoveries*, Vol. 5, pp. 218-20.)

[*Unity*, February (?) 1900]

. . . . . .

. . . We had eight lectures at the Home by the Swami (This newspaper report is an overview of eight class lectures delivered at the Home of Truth in December 1899 and January 1900, of which there is only one verbatim transcript, "Hints on Practical Spirituality", published in Complete Works, II: 24-37.) and all were intensely interesting, though a few malcontents complained because he did not give some short cuts into the Kingdom [of Heaven] and show an easy way to the attainment of mental powers; instead he would say,

> Go home and promise yourself that you will not worry for a whole month even though the maid breaks all your best china.

There is combined in the Swami Vivekananda the learning of a university president, the dignity of an archbishop, with the grace and winsomeness of a free natural child. Getting on the platform without a moment's preparation he would soon be in the midst of his subject, sometimes becoming almost tragic as his mind would wander from deep metaphysics to the prevailing condition in Christian countries today who go and seek to reform Filipinos with the swords in one hand and the Bible in the other, or in South Africa allow children of the same father to cut each other to pieces. To contrast this condition of things he described what took place during the last famine in India where men would die of starvation beside their cattle rather than stretch forth a hand to kill. (Will Unity readers remember the fifty million Hindoos who are starving today and send them a blessing?)

Instead of trying to give much of what we heard from the Swami direct, I will append a few of the sayings of his master, Ramakrishna, that will better indicate the nature of his teaching. His chief aim seems to be to encourage people in living simple, quiet wholesome lives — that the life shall be the religion, not something separate and apart.

To the true mother he gives the highest place, counting her as more to be esteemed than those who simply run around teaching. "Anyone can talk," he said,

> but if I had to look after a baby, I could not endure existence for more than three days.

Frequently he would speak of the "mother" as we speak of the "father," and would say "the mother will take care of us," or "the mother will look after things."

We had a lecture on Christmas day from the Swami entitled, "Christ's Mission to the World," and a better one on this subject I never heard. No Christian minister could have presented Jesus as a character worthy (of) the greatest reverence more eloquently or more powerfully than did this learned Hindoo, who told us that in this country on account of his dark skin he has been refused admission to hotels, and even barbers have sometimes objected to shave him. Is it any wonder that our "heathen" brethren never fail to make mention of this fact that even "our" Master was an Oriental?

Hindoo Monk Lectures

(*New Discoveries*, Vol. 5, pp. 315-16.)

[San Francisco Chronicle, February 24, 1900]

Swami Vivekananda's Topic Is "The Idea of Universal Religion"

At Golden Gate Hall last evening Swami Vivekananda, a Hindoo mon entertained an audience for an hour and a half with his lecture on "The Ide of Universal Religion." (Of which no verbatim transcript is available.) . . .

Tracing religion from the commencement of history he spoke of th existence of creeds. Sects were known from the earliest time, he said. A time rolled on there began various contests for a supremacy between th various sects. History, he declared, was a mere repetition of slaughter unde the guise of religion. Superstition, he thought, was fast becoming a thin of the past through the expansion of the minds of men. They had mo liberality of thought now. They were deeper students of philosophy an through the principles of true philosophy only could religion in its deepe form be found. Until men could accord to others the right of free belief c all subjects, and be willing to believe truth under whatever form it mig appear, no universal religion would be manifest to the world, he declared. would never be promulgated by any society, but would grow instinctive as the intellect of man developed.

Vedantism, And What It Is And What It Is Not

(*New Discoveries*, Vol. 5, pp. 329-31.)

Lecture of Swami Vivekananda on the Religion of the Hindoos

[*Oakland Tribune*, February 26, 1900]

It is the Only Creed, He Says, that Can Be Taught Without Lies and Without Compromise

The claims of the Brahmin religion, or Vedantism, on the modern world were presented to-night at the Congress of Religions in the First Unitarian Church by Swami Vivekananda, (The lecture was entitled "The Claims of Vedanta on the Modern World", of which there is no verbatim transcript available. Cf. Complete Works, VIII: 231-34 for a somewhat different report, which does not include most of the Swami's direct quotes appearing in the *Oakland Tribune* .) a remarkably eloquent expounder of that faith. . . .

To his auditors to-night he explained Vedantism as the religion of the Vedas, or ancient Hindoo books, which, he asserted, is "the mother of religion."

"It may seem ridiculous how a book can be without beginning or end," he said,

True Religion

(*New Discoveries*, Vol. 6, pp. 405-6.)

[*The Alameda Encinal*, April 5, 1900]

Hindu Philosopher Gives His Ideas

Last evening the Swami Vivekananda gave the first of a series of three public lectures at Tucker Hall on "The Development of Religious Ideas." (Of which no verbatim transcript is available.)

The speaker dwelt briefly on the similarity of ideas in the minds of orthodox Christians, Mohammedans and Hindus with regard to the origin of their religions. Each believed his particular prophet or teacher to have been inspired in some mysterious way by a God or Gods, who as it were, regulated or influenced the affairs of this world from a distance. The modern scientific mind, on the contrary, instead of seeking for outside or supernatural causes for phenomena endeavored to find cause in the thing or condition itself.

While at first glance this method of investigation might seem to take from religion some of its vital elements, yet in reality it resulted in man finding that the spiritual attributes of deity and the states of mind producing heaven and hell were all within himself, and although the result of this rational modern inquiry might appear to contradict much that had been handed down in the old religious writings such as Bible, Koran and Vedas, yet the contradiction was more apparent than real, for the prophets and teachers of old had true perceptions, but were mistaken only in attributing their experiences to outside agencies, instead of realizing them to be the development and expression of elements in their own souls before unknown and unrecognized.

The lecturer traced some of the common beliefs regarding location of heavens and hells, of various burial rites and customs, and he spoke of the impressions made on the primitive mind that resulted in a personification of the active natural forces in the phenomena with which we are surrounded. . . .

Swami Vivekananda On Love

(*New Discoveries*, Vol. 3, pp. 237-40.)

[*Maidenhead Adviser*, October 23, 1895]

On Thursday the Swami Vivekananda delivered a lecture at the Town Hall, Maidenhead, taking as his subject "The Eastern Doctrine of Love." Owing to other attractions in the town the attendance was not large. Many of the public also associated the lecturer with the Theosophical Society, with which, however, he has, we are informed, nothing whatever to do, nor with any other society, neither does he propose forming any society himself. He believes in expounding his views to whoever will listen to them and leaving those individuals to advocate them as a whole, or with whatever modifications they may deem fitting, or to reject them altogether, believing that out of the strife of all opinions truth at length prevails.

The chair was taken at 8 p.m. by Mr. E. Gardner, J.P., C.C., and he very briefly introduced the lecturer, who was clad in his native costume. The Swami then proceeded to express his view upon devotion to deity, or, as more commonly expressed in the East — love (Bhakti), to the following effect: — Religion may be divided into two forms, the first almost entirely superstitious and the second merely metaphysical, but if either of these is to have any force it must be accompanied by love. Work alone without this element did not satisfy. The land might be covered with hospitals, penetrated by good roads; there might be great social institutions well conducted, and good sanitation, but these were all external physical processes and by themselves brought man no nearer to Divinity. Both the realist and the idealist were necessary and complementary one of the other. The idealist brought the bold aspiration down to earth, the realist caused it to take form through work. Love cannot be defined in positive terms, only negatively. Its nature is of the form of renunciation. In its more general sense it might be divided threefold: (1) That love which is for one's own pleasure, irrespective of pleasure or pain to others — the purely selfish, the lowest. (2) That love which exchanges — "I will love you if you love me. We will make each other mutually happy" — the partially selfish, the middle path trodden by the great majority of mankind. (3) That love which gives all and asks for nothing, without premeditation and which never regrets, unconquerable by any evil thing done to him from whom it emanates. It is the highest, the divine. Only with this last kind are we concerned here. The first is the path of the sensualist and the animal, the second the path of struggling humanity on its way to better things, the third the real path of love, trodden by those who renounce the world and set out upon that road which leads to Eternal Peace. In that love there is no fear. Love kills fear. A lion might stand over a babe and threaten its life; the mother knows no fear, she does not fly, but she opposes. At that moment love destroys terror; at other times the same woman would run from a small dog. A fierce Mahomedan [*sic*] warrior went to a garden to pray. In the same garden a girl had appointed to meet her lover. The warrior lay prostrate on his face according to the prescribed form of his religion. At that moment the girl espied her lover, and with joy rushing to meet him, trod upon the prostrate form. He jumped up and laying hand upon his sword would have slain the girl. "How dare you?" cried he, "vile wench, disturb my worship, my devotion to God, with your base feet." "Worship! devotion!" cried the girl, "you do not know what they are. You had no devotion, lying there, no spirit of worship. If I, a timid girl, could so forget the presence of an object of dread like you, in my worship and devotion to my earthly lover as to tread upon you and not even know it, how much more should you, if your heart had been absorbed in love and devotion to God, have been ignorant that I touched you?" The warrior was humbled and appeased and went away. Our highest ideal of love is the image which we form for ourselves of deity. A barbarous people have a tyrannical and cruel god. A wise and noble people see God in ever and ever widening potencies. God is always God, but the views which men and nations may take of Him vary. No higher view is known than that of love. The man who bears in his heart an unrelaxing love to every creature, whether he recognise that that creature is a manifestation of God, in which he is actually present, or whether he look upon it merely as fashioned by Deity, that man is on the path to Deity, on the great path of devotion and renunciation. He cannot injure the creature of God, however repulsive to his narrower view of what should or should not be. He gives in love, not in pride; in loving Deity he loves its manifestations, works with them and abides by them.

The lecture was impressively delivered, and at the close a vote of thanks was accorded the Chairman (on the proposition of Mr. E. T. Sturdy, of Caversham).

The proceedings occupied only a little over half an hour.

An Indian Ascetic

(*New Discoveries*, Vol. 3, pp. 246-47.)

[*Standard*, October 23, 1895]

Since the days of Ramahoun [Ram Mohan] Roy, says the Standard, with the single exception of Keshub Chunder [Keshab Chandra] Sen, there has not appeared on an English platform a more interesting Indian figure than the Brahman who lectured in Princes' [Prince's] Hall last night. . . .

The lecture was a most fearless and eloquent exposition of the pantheistic philosophy of the Vedanta school, and the Swami seems to have incorporated into his system a good deal also of the moral element of the Yoga school, as the closing passage of his lecture presented in a modified form not the advocacy of mortification, which is the leading feature of the latter school, but the renunciation of all so-called material comforts and blessings, as the only means of entering into perfect union with the supreme and absolute Self. The opening passages of the lecture were a review of the rise of the grosser form of Materialism in the beginning of the present century, and the later development of the various forms of metaphysical thought, which for a time swept materialism away. From this he passed on to discuss the origin and nature of knowledge. In some respects his views on this point were almost a statement of pure Fichteism, but they were expressed in language, and they embodied illustrations, and made admissions which no German transcendentalist would have used. He admitted there was a gross material world outside, but he confessed he did not know what matter was. He asserted that mind was a finer matter, and that behind was the soul of man, which was immovable, fixed, before which outward objects passed, as it were, in a procession, which was without beginning or end — in other words, which was eternal, and finally which was God. He worked out this pantheistic conception of the personal identity of man and God with great comprehensiveness and an ample wealth of illustration, and in passage after passage of great beauty, solemnity, and earnestness. "There is only one Soul in the Universe", he said:

> There is no "you" or "me"; all variety is merged into the absolute unity, the one infinite existence — God.

From this, of course, followed the immortality of the soul, and something like the transmigration of souls towards higher manifestations of perfection. As already stated, his peroration of twenty minutes was a statement of the doctrine of renunciation. In the course of it he made some remorselessly disparaging criticism on the work that factories, engines and other inventions, and books were doing for man, compared with half a dozen words spoken by Buddha or Jesus. The lecture was evidently quite extemporaneous, and was delivered in a pleasing voice, free from any kind of hesitation.

Native Indian Lecturer At Princes' Hall

(*New Discoveries*, Vol. 3, p. 248.)

[*London Morning Post*, October 23, 1895]

— Last night at Princes' [Prince's] Hall, Piccadilly, Swami Vivekananda, an Indian Yogi, who is at present on a visit to this country, delivered what was described as an "oration" on the subject of "Self Knowledge." (Of which no verbatim transcript is available. Cf. the preceding newspaper report 'An Indian Ascetic', pp 515-16, for another report of the same lecture, delivered October 22, 1895.) A Yogi, it was explained, is one who formally renounces the world and gives himself up to study and devotion. Swami Vivekananda originally left his native land for the purpose of giving his interpretation of the Vedanta philosophy at the Parliament of Religions which was held two years ago at Chicago, and since that time he has been engaged in delivering lectures on the same subject in America. In the course of his address last night he declared that there were indications in these closing days of the 19th century that the pendulum of scientific thought was swinging back, for men all over the world were rummaging in the pages of ancient records, and ancient religious forms were again coming to the fore. To many this seemed to be a case of degeneration, while others regarded it as one of those outbursts of superstition which periodically visited society, but to the scientific student there was in the present state of things a prognostication of grand future benefit. The lecturer then proceeded at considerable length to describe the peculiar system of philosophy which he teaches, and traced the three different stages of the religion which has grown out of it. He spoke with a good deal of fluency, and his remarks were listened to with attention by the somewhat small audience.

The Christian Commonwealth

(*New Discoveries*, Vol. 3, pp. 267-69.)

[*Christian Commonwealth*, November 14, 1895]

South Place Chapel Lecture

"The Swami Vivekananda" enlightened the congregation at South-pla Chapel last Sunday morning on "The Basis of Vedanta Morality." (A lectu delivered in London, England, on November 10, 1895, of which there is verbatim transcript available.) . . .

The Swami explained that in the system of morality which he w expounding actions were not inspired by any hope of reward, here hereafter, nor by any fear of punishment in this world or in the beyond: "W must work simply from the impetus within, work for work's sake, duty duty's sake." This idea of morality is claimed to be superior to the religi of Jesus, and so has beguiled some so-called Christians into Buddhism other Eastern philosophies. But the essence of true Christianity is that your actions are inspired by the heavenly kingdom within you, Parad will be the result, whereas, if you act in harmony with the devil's kingdo without you will land in Perdition. The genuine Christian does not, as t Swami seemed to suggest, act for the purpose of evading punishments, b at the same time he sees the ultimate consequences of all actions. . . .

An Universal Religion

(*New Discoveries*, Vol. 3, pp. 276-77.)

[*The Queen, The Lady's Newspaper, November 23, 1895*]

Mrs. Haweis's first autumn At home took place last Saturday at Queen's House, when the Indian Yogi, or ascetic, Swami Vive Kananda (Buddhist [*sic*] delegate at the Parliament of Religions at Chicago in 1893) discussed in a liberal spirit, and not without humour, the chances and the charms of an universal religion. He showed that the underlying principles of all the great religions of the world resembled one another, and amongst the great prophets he placed the Christian Redeemer very high, implying, however, that His teaching was little borne out sometimes by His professed followers. There was no radical impossibility of reconciliation between sects, now biting and devouring each other from the best motives, if charity and sympathy were carried into the kiosque, the temple, and the church. Canon Basil Wilberforce and the Rev. H. R. Haweis both made interesting speeches in reply to the Swami. . . . The guests numbered 150.

Education*

(*New Discoveries*, Vol. 4, p. 157.)

[*Daily Chronicle*, May 14, 1896]

The Sesame Club. — At a meeting of the Sesame Club on Tuesday night [May 12], the chairman, Mr. Ashton Jonson, said he regretted to announce that Mrs. Norman was too unwell to be present to open, as announced, a debate on "Should we return to the land." An address was accordingly given by Swami Vivekananda on the subject of education, (There is no verbatim transcript available. Cf. the Indian newspaper report "On Education", p. 535.) in which he urged that no one could obtain intellectual greatness until he was physically pure. Morality gave strength; the immoral were always weak, and could never raise themselves intellectually, much less spiritually. Directly [as] immorality began to enter the national life its foundations commenced to rot. As the life blood of every nation was to be found in the schools, where boys and girls were receiving their education, it was absolutely essential that the young students should be pure, and this purity must be taught them.

Spiritualism And The Vedanta Philosophy

(*New Discoveries*, Vol. 4, pp. 229-30.)

[*Light*, July 4, 1896]

When first we heard that the Swami Vivekananda was coming to London to expound the Vedanta Philosophy, we were hopeful that his teaching would not only confirm the faith of Spiritualists, but might also add to their number. We hoped this, because the very essence of the Hindu Philosophy is that man is a spirit, and *has* a body, and not that man *is* a body, and may have a spirit also; which is as far as many a Western mind can reach. . . .

It has been the glorious privilege of our modern Spiritualism to prove by actual demonstration the existence of spirit apart from flesh, and it would, therefore, seem reasonable to look for co-operation on the part of the exponents of the Vedanta Philosophy and the supporters of Spiritualism. We are not quite certain, however, that this desirable consummation can be attained, for observations made very recently by the Swami are calculated only to divide the two sects. The Vedanta Philosophy sets before the student an ideal aim! Nothing less, in fact, than the unfolding of the God within him, and nothing could well be more impressive and inspiring than the presentation of this idea by a speaker of the force and eloquence of the Swami. We could only respect and admire, until modern Spiritualism was alluded to, and that in a manner which left upon us the impression that the Swami condemned without reservation all sitting for phenomena. He admitted having sat for observation with professional mediums, and held that one and all had practised fraud. "Spirit voices," according to the Swami, are never heard to clash! As the "sepulchral dies away the small child's voice rises up," intimating thus that ventriloquism was invariably responsible for the sounds. "Spirit messages," he remarked,

> were quite worthless, for they never rose above the level of "I am well and happy," or "Give John a piece of cake."

This assertion could, of course, only be made in ignorance of the contents of "Spirit Teachings," a book which, we think, can well stand comparison even with the exalted teaching of the Swami Vivekananda. The process of making up sham materialisations and working the figure on the end of a wire was also described in detail.

We were present again the following evening, when a paper of questions bearing upon the adverse criticism of the Swami was read out to the meeting. Some thirty minutes were then passed in qualifying and explaining his remarks of the night before, and, to our deep satisfaction, the Swami not only confessed his belief in the possibility of spirits communicating with mortals, but even expressed his conviction that at times spirits of a high grade visited earth in order to assist mankind. It is, however, we conceive, no part of the Vedanta Philosophy to recommend the seeking of such intercourse, on account of its possible "dangers." It is commonly held that the undeveloped spirit can most easily communicate with man, consequently the Swami uttered his word of warning and withheld any word of encouragement. . . .

An October Class Review

(*New Discoveries*, Vol. 4, pp. 370-71.)
[*Light*, October 28, 1896]

On the sixth floor of one of the dismal but convenient Victoria-street houses, we lately listened to a discourse by Swami Vivekananda — one of a long series on the Hindoo Religion and Philosophy. . . . For an hour and a half he spoke, without a note. It is true that the discourse was rather a flow of remarks than a connected study, but it was all keenly interesting.

The subject, in the main, was the Vedas, but we got excursions upon Evolution, Modern Science, Idealism and Realism, the Supremacy of Spirit, &c. On the whole, we gathered that the speaker was a preacher of the universal religion of spiritual ascendency and spiritual harmony. Certain passages from the Vedas — beautifully translated and read, by the way — were charming in their bearing upon the humanness and sharp reality of a life beyond the veil. One longed for more of this.

We were much impressed with the admission that in the Vedas there were many contradictions, and that devout Hindoos never thought of denying them nor reconciling them. Everyone was free to take what he liked. At different stages and on different planes, all were true. Hence the Hindoos never excommunicated and never persecuted. The contradictions in the Vedas are like the contradictions in life — they are very real, but they are all true. This seems impossible, but there is sound sense in it. At all events, as regards excommunication and persecution, we only wish the Christians could make the Hindoo's claim.

A Bengali Sadhu

[*Madura Mail*, January 28, 1893]

A BENGALI SADHU ON HINDU
RELIGION AND SOCIOLOGY

A young Bengalee Sanyashi [Sannyâsin] of about thirty-two years of age, and a Master of Arts of the Calcutta University was last week interviewed at the Triplicane Literary Society by about a hundred educated Indians among whom was Dewan Bahadur Raghunatha Rao. A summary of what was stated by the Sadhu is published by the *Indian Social Reformer*, from which we make the following extracts:

The Vedic Religion

The perfect religion is the Vedic religion. The Vedas have two parts, mandatory and optional. The mandatory injunctions are eternally binding on us. They constitute the Hindu religion. The optional ones are not so. These have been changing and been changed by the Rishis to suit the times. The Brahmins at one time ate beef and married Sudras. [A] calf was killed to please a guest. Sudras cooked for Brahmins. The food cooked by a male Brahmin was regarded as polluted food. But we have changed our habits to suit the present yug[a]. Although our caste rules have so far changed from the time of Manu, still if he should come to us now, he would still call us Hindus. Caste is a social organization and not a religious one. It was the outcome of the natural evolution of our society. It was found necessary and convenient at one time. It has served its purpose. But for it, we would long ago have become Mahomedans [sic]. It is useless now. It may be dispensed with. Hindu religion no longer requires the prop of the caste system. A Brahmin may interdine with anybody, even a Pariah. He won't thereby lose his spirituality. A degree of spirituality that is destroyed by the touch of a Pariah, is a very poor quantity. It is almost at the zero point. Spirituality of a Brahmin must overflow, blaze and burn [so] as to warm into spiritual life not one Pariah but thousands of Pariahs who may touch him. The old Rishis observed no distinctions or restrictions as regards food. A man who feels that his own spirituality is so flimsy that the sight of a low caste man annihilates it need not approach a Pariah and must keep his precious little to himself.

The Hindu Ideal of Life

The Hindu Ideal of life is "Nivarti" [Nivritti]. (Nivritti and Parvritti are key concepts in Hindu philosophy, and Swami Vivekananda has frequently interpreted and elaborated on them (e.g., see Karma-Yoga, Ch. VI) in their traditional connotations. But the interpretation of the terms here ascribed to him by the Indian Social Reformer's reporter is not in accord with what the Swami has said elsewhere.) Nivarti means subjugation and conquest of evil passions, of *Tamasa* nature of lust, revenge and avarice. It does not mean conquest of all desire. It means only the annihilation of gross desires. Every man is bound to love and sympathize with his fellow-creatures. [A] Sanyasi is one who has vanquished all his selfish passions and vowed to devote his life for the good of others. He loves all. "Pravirti" [Pravritti] means love of God and all his creatures. Sanyasis ought to be fed. They are not like the Christian bishops and Archbishops who must be paid to do their work with thousands of pounds per annum; all whose earnings are spent upon their own luxury — their wife and children. [The] Sanyasi wants only a morsel of food, and then he places all his knowledge and services at the disposal of the public. He is a wandering missionary. Individuals and society have to work themselves up from "brute through man, into divine". Even the lowest of the Hindus, the Pariah, has less of the brute in him than a Briton in a similar social status. This is the result of an old and excellent religious civilization. This evolution to a higher spiritual state is possible only through discipline and education.

The Shradh [Shrâddha] Ceremony

Every institution, caste, early marriage etc., that stands in the way of education, ought at once to be knocked on the head. Even "Shradh" may be given up, if the performance of it involves waste of time which might be better used for self-education. But "Shradh" should not be given up. The meaning of the Mantras is very edifying. The Mantras depict the suffering and care undergone by our parents on our behalf. The performance of it is an honour paid to the memory of the sum total of the spirit of our forefathers, whose virtues we inherit. Shradh has nothing to do with one's salvation. Yet no Hindu who loves his religion, his country and his past great men should give up Shradh. The outward formalities and the feeding of the Brahmins are not essential. We have no Brahmins in these days worthy of being fed on Shradh days. The Brahmins fed ought not to be professional eaters, but Brahmins who feed disciples *gratis*, and teach them true Vedic doctrines. In these days, Shradh may be performed mentally.

Education of Women

The jealous guardianship of our women shows that we Hindus have declined in our national virtues, that we reverted to the "brutal state". Every man must so discipline his mind as to bring himself to regard all women as his sisters or mothers. Women must have freedom to read, to receive as good an education as men. Individual development is impossible with ignorance and slavery.

Emancipation of the Hindus

Through the slavery of a thousand years, Hindus have at present degenerated. They have forgotten their own self-respect. Every English boy is taught to feel his importance, he thinks that he is a member of a great race, the conquerors of the Earth. The Hindu feels from his boyhood just the reverse that he is born to slave. We can't become a great nation unless we love our religion and try to respect ourselves, and respect our country men and society. The Hindus of modern times are generally hypocrites. They must rise, and combine the faith in the true Vedic religion, with a knowledge of the political and scientific truths of the Europeans. The evils of caste seem to be more prevalent in the South than in Bengal. In Bengal a Brahmin uses the water touched by the Sudras, but here the Sudra is kept at a great distance by the Brahmin. There are no Brahmins in [the] Kali Yug[a]. The Pariahs, our fellow beings, ought to be educated by the higher castes, must [. . .] truths of Hindu religion and be [. . .] Brahmins. The first duty of a Brahmin is to love all. There must first be an amalgamation of the Brahmins, then of all the Dwijas, and then of the Dwijas and Sudras.

The Parliament Of Religions

(*Vivekananda in Indian Newspapers, p. 4.*)

BY H. R. HAWEIS

[*The Indian Mirror (from The Daily Chronicle),*

November 28, 1893]

. . . Vivekananda, the popular Hindu monk, whose physiognomy bore the most striking resemblance to the classic face of the Buddha, denounced our commercial prosperity, our bloody wars, and our religious intolerance, declaring that at such a price the "mild Hindu" would have none of our vaunted civilisation. . . . "You come," he cried,

> with the Bible in one hand and the conqueror's sword in the other — you, with your religion of yesterday, to us, who were taught thousands of years ago by our *Rishis* precepts as noble and lives as holy as your Christ's. You trample on us and treat us like the dust beneath your feet. You destroy precious life in animals. You are *carnivores*. You degrade our people with drink. You insult our women. You scorn our religion — in many points like yours, only better, because more humane. And then you wonder why Christianity makes such slow progress in India. I tell you it is because you are not like your Christ, whom we could honour and reverence. Do you think, if you came to our doors like him, meek and lowly, with a message of love, living and working and suffering for others, as he did, we should turn a deaf ear? Oh no! We should receive him and listen to him, and as we have done our own inspired *Rishis* (teachers). . . .

Parliament Of Religions In Chicago

(Vivekananda in Indian Newspapers, pp. 5-6.)

[*The Indian Mirror*, December 7, 1893]

HINDU CRITICISES CHRISTIANITY

MR.VIVEKANUNDA SAYS
RELIGION OF THE VEDAS

IS RELIGION OF LOVE

VIVEKANUNDA SAYS CHRISTIANITY
IS INTOLERANT

Dr. Noble presided at the afternoon session. The Hall of Colombus [Columbus] was badly crowded. . . . Dr. Noble then presented Swami Vivekananda, the Hindu monk, who was applauded loudly as he stepped forward to the centre of the platform. He wore an orange robe, bound with a scarlet sash, and a pale yellow turban. The customary smile was on his handsome face and his eyes shown with animation. Said he:

> We who come from the East have sat here on the platform day after day, and have been told in a patronizing way that we ought to accept Christianity because Christian nations are the most prosperous. We look about us, and we see England, the most prosperous Christian nation in the world, with her foot on the neck of 250,000,000 of Asiatics. We look back into history, and see that the prosperity of Christian Europe began with Spain. Spain's prosperity began with the invasion of Mexico. Christianity wins its prosperity by cutting the throats of its fellowmen. At such a price the Hindu will not have prosperity. (Vide "Cantakerous Remarks", Complete Works, III: 474.)

> I have sat here to-day, and I have heard the height of intolerance. I have heard the creed of the Moslem applauded, when to-day the Moslem sword is carrying destruction into India. Blood and the sword are not for the Hindu, whose religion is based on the law of love. (This last paragraph is a heretofore unpublished extract.)

When the applause had ceased, Mr. Vivekananda went [on] to read his paper, a summary of which follows: [*Vide* "Paper on Hinduism", *Complete Works*, I: 6-20]. . . .

On Christian Conversion

(*Vivekananda in Indian Newspapers, p.* 25.)

[*The Indian Mirror*, June 14, 1894]

There has been some lively correspondence between Swami Vivekanand and a retired Christian Missionary on the work and prospects of Christianity in India. Among other things, the Swami is reported to have said that "the way of converting is absolutely absurd";

> Missionary doctors do no good, because they are not in touch with the people. . . . They accomplish nothing in the way of converting, although they may have nice sociable times among themselves, &c.

The reverend gentleman took exception to the words, maintaining that speaking the vernaculars well, nobody of foreigners understands, and sympathises with Indians better than Missionaries. The Missionaries are undoubtedly good and well-meaning people; but we think, the statement of the Swami that they are seldom in touch with the people, is not without foundation. With the revival of Hinduism, manifested in every part of the country, it is doubtful whether Christianity will have any sway over the Hindus. The present is a critical time for Christian Missions in India. The Swami thanked the Missionary for calling him his fellow-countryman. "This is the first time," he wrote,

> any European foreigner, born in India though he be, has dared to call a detested Native by that name — Missionary or no Missionary. Would you dare call me the same in India?

. . . . .

The Central Idea Of The Vedas

(*Vivekananda in Indian Newspapers, p. 30.*)

[*The Indian Mirror*, July 20, 1894]

Swami Vivekananda explained in America the central idea of the Vedas as follows:

> I humbly beg to differ from those who see in monotheism, in the recognition of a personal God, apart from Nature, the acme of intellectual development. I believe, it is only a kind of anthropomorphism which the human mind stumbles upon in its first efforts to understand the unknown. The ultimate satisfaction of human reason and custom lies in the realisation of that universal essence which is the All. And I hold an irrefragable evidence that this idea is present in the Vedas, the numerous gods and their invocations notwithstanding. This idea of formless All, the *Sat*, i.e., esse or being, called *Atman* and *Brahman* in the Upanishads, and further explained in the Darsans, is the central idea of the Vedas, nay, the root-idea of the Hindu religion in general. (Unidentified source.)

Swami Vivekananda On The Sea-Voyage Movement

(Vivekananda in Indian Newspapers, pp. 260-62.)

[*The Bengalee*, May 18, 1895]

There is not a Hindoo who is not proud of Vivekananda Swami – who would not honor him and his teachings. He has done honor to himself, to his race and his religion. If we are right in this view, it follows that the opinions of Vivekananda are entitled to the highest consideration. This is what he says with regard to the sea-voyage movement: –

> Expansion is life; contraction is death. Love is life, hatred is death. We began to die the day we began to contract – to hate other races – and nothing can prevent our death, until we come back to life, to expansion. We must mix, therefore, with all the races of the earth and every Hindoo that goes out to travel in foreign parts, does more benefit to his country than hundreds of those bundles of superstition and selfishness whose one aim in life is to be the dog in the manger. Those wonderful structures of national life which the Western nations have raised are supported by pillars of character – and until we can produce such by the hundred, it is useless to fret and fume against this power or that power. Does anyone deserve liberty who is not ready to give it to others? Let us calmly and in manly fashion go to work – instead of dissipating our energies in unnecessary frettings and fumings and I, for one, thoroughly believe that no power in the universe can withhold from anyone anything he really deserves. The past was great no doubt, but I sincerely believe that the future in store is glorious still. (Vide Complete Works, IV: 366.)

We must mix with other nations and take from them whatever good they have to give us. It is our exclusiveness, our unwillingness to learn from foreign nations which is mainly responsible for our present degradation. We considered ourselves to be the elect of heaven, and superior to the nations of the earth in all respects. We regarded them as barbarians, their touch as pollution, their knowledge as worse than ignorance. We lived in a world of our own creation. We would teach the foreigner nothing — we would learn nothing from the foreigner. At last the disillusion came. The foreigner became our master — the arbiter of our destinies. We eagerly took to his learning. We found that there was much in it that was novel, much that was highly useful. We found that so far as the material comforts of life were concerned the foreigner vastly out-distanced us — that his control over the powers of nature was far greater than any we had dreamt of. He had annihilated time and space, and had subordinated the powers of nature to the convenience of man. He had many wonderful things to teach us. We learnt them eagerly. But still we don't visit his country. If we do, we lose caste. We are under a foreign Government. We eagerly study a foreign language and literature and admire all that is good and beautiful in it. We use foreign articles for dress and consumption. But still we dare not visit the country of our rulers, for fear of excommunication. Against this unmeaning prejudice, the great Swami, who is a Hindoo of Hindoos, indignantly raises his voice of protest. The objectors, in his expressive language, are like the dog in the manger. They will not travel to foreign countries, — they will not allow others to travel. Yet the fact remains, says the Swami, that these travelled Hindoos do more benefit to their country than

> hundreds of those bundles of superstition and selfishness, whose one aim in life is to be like the dog in the manger. (Vide Complete Works, *IV: 366*.)

. . . . . .

If we had our *Rishis* in this age, as we had them in the ages that are gone by, we are sure they would have withdrawn the interdiction to sea-voyage, if indeed any such interdiction has been laid in the past. Society is an organism which obeys the immutable law of progress; and change, judicious and cautious change, is necessary for the well-being, and indeed the preservation of the social system. However that may be, it is something to know that so high an authority and so good a Hindoo as Swami Vivekananda supports travel to foreign countries. . . .

A Summary Of "Buddhism, The Fulfilment Of Hinduism"

(*Vivekananda in Indian Newspapers, p. 73.*)

[*The Indian Mirror*, June 29, 1895]

Swami Vivekananda's speech, delivered in Chicago at the presentatic of the Buddhists on September 26, 1893, is published in MacNeely's editic of the "History of the Parliament of Religions". The following were h concluding words: —

> We cannot live without you, nor you without us. Then believe that separation has shown to us, that you cannot stand without the brain and the philosophy of the Brahman [sic], nor we without your heart. This separation between the Buddhist and the Brahman [Brahmin] is the cause of the downfall of India. That is why India has been the slave of conquerors for the past 1000 years. Let us then join the wonderful intellect of the Brahman [Brahmin] with the heart, the noble soul, the wonderful humanising power of the Great Master. (Vide "Buddhism, the Fulfilment of Hinduism", Complete Works, I: 21-23, for a somewhat different summary paragraph.)

Indian Philosophy And Western Society

(Vivekananda in Indian Newspapers, pp. 85-86.)

[*The Indian Mirror*, December 1, 1895]

At the weekly meeting of the Balloon Society, an address on "Man and Society in the Light of Vedanta" was given by Swami Vivekananda. The Swami who wore the red robe of his sect, spoke with great fluency and in perfect English for more than an hour without the help of a single note. He said that religion was the most wonderful factor in the social organism. If knowledge was the highest gain that science could give, what could be greater than the knowledge of God, of the soul, of man's own nature which was given by the study of religion? It was not only impossible that there should be one religion for the whole world, but it would be dangerous. If the whole of religious thought was at the same level, it would be the death of religious thought; variety was its life. There were four types of religion — (1) the worker, (2) the emotional, (3) the mystical, and (4) the philosophical. Each man unfortunately became so wedded to his own type that he had no eyes to see what existed in the world. He struggled to make others of the same type. That religion would be perfect which gave scope to all the different characters. The Vedantic religion took in all, and each could choose in what his nature required. A discussion followed.

Swami Vivekananda In America

(Vivekananda in Indian Newspapers, pp. 89-90.)

[The Indian Mirror (from the New York Herald),

March 25, 1896]

Many well-known persons are seeking to follow the teaching of Swami Vivekananda's Philosophy.

. . . . . .

A Lecture by the Swami

Swami Vivekananda sat in the centre, clad in an ochre coloured robe. The Hindu had his audience divided on either side of him and there was between fifty and a hundred persons present. The class was in Karma-Yoga, which has been described as the realisation of one's self as God through works and duty.

Its theme was: —

"That which ye sow ye reap", whether of good or evil.

Following the lecture or instruction the Swami held an informal reception, and the magnetism of the man was shown by the eager manner in which those who had been listening to him hastened to shake hands or begged for the favour of an introduction. But concerning himself the Swami will not say more than is absolutely necessary. Contrary to the claim made by some of his pupils he declares that he has come to this country alone and not so officially representing any order of Hindu monks. He belongs to the Sanyasis he will say; and is hence free to travel without losing his caste. When it is pointed out to him that Hinduism is not a proselytising religion, he says he has a message to the West as Buddha had a message to the East. (Vide Complete Works, *V: 314.*) When questioned concerning the Hindu religion, and asked whether he intends to introduce its practices and ritual into [t]his country, he declares that he is preaching simply philosophy.

On Education*

(Vivekananda in Indian Newspapers, p. 101.)

[*The Indian Mirror*, June 19, 1896]

Swami Saradananda in a letter from London written to the Editor of the *Brahmavadin* says: —

Swami Vivekananda has made a very good beginning here. A large number of the people attend his classes regularly, and the lectures are most interesting. Canon Haweis, one of the leaders of the Anglican Church, came the other day, and was much interested. He saw the Swami before, in the Chicago fairs, and loved him from that time. On Tuesday last, the Swami lectured on "Education" at the Sesame Club. It is a respectable club got up by women for diffusing female education. In this he dealt with the old educational system of India, pointed out clearly and impressively that, the sole aim of the system was "man-making" and not cramming and compared it with the present system. He held that, the mind of the man is an infinite reservoir of knowledge, and all knowledge, present, past or future, is within man, manifested or non-manifested, and the object of every system of education should be to help the mind to manifest it. For instance, the law of gravitation was within man, and the fall of the apple helped Newton to think upon it, and bring it out from within his mind. His class days have been arranged as follows: —

Tuesdays, morning and evening; Thursdays, morning and evening; Friday, evening question classes. So the Swami has to do four lectures, and one class on questions every week. In the class lecture, he has begun with Gnan [Jnâna-]Yoga. A short-hand report of these lectures is being taken down by Mr. Goodwin, who is a great admirer of the Swami, and these lectures will be published later on.

The Swami Vivekananda In England

(Vivekananda in Indian Newspapers, pp. 493-95.)

[*The Brahmavadin*, July 18, 1896]

SIR,

I feel sure you will be glad to have an idea of the progress of the Swami's work in England, as a supplement to the letter which the Swami Saradananda sent you a few weeks ago. At that time a series of Sunday lectures was being arranged, and three of these have now been given. They are held in one of the galleries of the Royal Institute of Painters in water colours, 191 Piccadilly, and have been so far remarkably successful in attaining their object, that of reaching people who, from one reason or another, cannot attend the class talks. The first of the series was "The Necessity of Religion". (Cf. Mr. J. J. Goodwin's published transcript "The Necessity of Religion", Complete Works, II: 57-69.) The Swami claimed that religion is and has been the greatest force in moulding the destinies of the human race. Concerning its origin he said that either of the two theories, (1) Spirit origin, (2) Search after the infinite, will meet the case, and, to his mind, neither contradicts the other, because the search after the departed of the Egyptians and Babylonians, and the attempt to peep behind the veil of the dawn, the evening, the thunderstorm, or other natural phenomena, of the Aryans, can both be included as a search after the super-sensuous, and therefore the unlimited. This unlimited, in the course of time became abstracted, first as a person, then as a presence, and lastly as the essence of all existence. To his mind the dream state is the first suggestion of religious inquiry, and inasmuch as the awakened state has always been, and always will be accompanied by the dream state, a suggestion of existence finer than that of the awakened state yet vanishing during it, the human mind will always be predisposed in favour of spiritual existence and a future life. It is in our dream-state that we really find, in a sense, our immortality. Later on, as dreams are found to be only milder manifestations of the awakened state, the search for still deeper planes of the mind begin[s], the super-conscious state of the mind. All religions claim to be founded on facts discovered in this state. The two important points to consider in this connection are, that all facts discovered in this way are, in the highest sense, abstractions, and secondly, that there is a constant struggle in the race to come up to this ideal, and everything which thwarts our progress towards that we feel as a limitation. This struggle soon ends in the discovery that to find infinite happiness, or power, or knowledge, or any other infinity, through the senses, is impossible, and then the struggle for other channels of expansion begins, and we find the necessity of religion. The second lecture was upon the subject "A Universal Religion", (No verbatim transcript available.) when the Swami gave, in substance, the lecture which most of your readers have seen in print as it was delivered in New York. As this lecture may be termed the Swami's "plan of campaign" we always await its delivery with very great interest, and it is most encouraging to note that the impression made here in London was equally as good as was the case when the lecture was delivered in the Hardman Hall, New York. The third of the series brought us up to Sunday last, June 21st, when "The Real and the Apparent Man" (Cf. Mr. J. J. Goodwin's published transcript "The Real Nature of Man", Complete Works, II: 70-87.) was the subject under discussion. In this the Swami, link by link, glanced over the thread of thought which has gradually advanced from the consideration of men as separate entities from God and the rest of the universe, up to the point at which we concede the impossibility of more than one Infinity, and the necessary consequence that which we now regard as men, as animals, as the universe of matter, cannot be the real unity; that the real must be something which is indivisible, and unchangeable; and when reason forces us to the conclusion that this phenomenal world can only be an illusion, through which we, as entities in the illusion, have to pass to discover our real nature, "That which exists is one; sages call it variously". But the Swami did not stop with the theory; he showed what would be the practical effect of such a theory, the gradual elimination from society of class distinctions, and distinctions between man and man, by greater unselfishness in the matters of money and power. Answering the objection that such a religion means loss of individuality, he argued that that which is changeful cannot be the real individuality, and that the gradual discovery of the reality behind us would mean the assumption of individuality and not its destruction.

The three lectures thus given have been so favorably received, and there have been so many wishes expressed for their continuation that three further lectures are to be given. . . .

Sincerely yours

A DISCIPLE (Probably Mr. E. T. Sturdy.)

(Correspondence)

63, St. George's Rd.

London, S. W.

June 23, 1896

On The Swiss Alps*

(Vivekananda in Indian Newspapers, p. 117.)

[*The Indian Mirror*, September 22, 1896]

Swami Vivekananda writes from Lake Luzern [Lucerne] Switzerland, under date the 23rd of August last. (Evidently an unpublished extract from one of the three (1, 2, 3) letters the Swami wrote from Lucerne (Vide "Epistles", Complete Works, V and VI).) He has been walking over several parts of the Cis-Alpine country, enjoying the pleasing views of nature there. He says that the scenery is in no respect less grand than that of the Himalayas. Still, he makes out two points of difference between the two mountainous regions. In the former the rapid and thick colonization has been marring the beauty of the place. In the latter, there has not yet been any such marked tendency. The former has become a resort mainly for the sanatorists and summer-residents; and the latter mainly for the pilgrims and devotees. The Swami is shortly going to visit Germany, where an interview will take place with Prof. Deussen, after which, by the 24th of September, he will go back to England. To India, most likely, as he says, he is returning by the next winter. He intends to reside in the Himalayas.

"The Ideal Of Universal Religion"

(Vivekananda in Indian Newspapers, pp. 331-33.)

[The Journal of the Maha-Bodhi Society, November 1896]

We have been presented with a copy of a booklet entitled the "Ideal of Universal Religion", published by the Brahmavadin Publishing Company, Madras. It is a lecture by Swami Vivekananda, delivered in America. The lecture is highly interesting and instructive. It is an attempt at a reconciliation between the diversity of religions. We hail the booklet as the symptom of the times, for it is evident for obvious reasons that men are beginning to awaken to the importance of this problem of religious harmony. Recently, in these countries leaders of different religious sects have attempted in their own way to reconcile this religious diversity, and have failed; they have aspired to defend their dogmas on the ground of distorted views of sectarianism. Swami Vivekananda has propounded a philosophical and at the same time a most practical solution of this problem of religious harmony. According to him, Vedanta is the bond between the ever conflicting religious differences. In the internal world, like the external world, there is also the centripetal and centrifugal action. We repel something, we attract something. Today we are attracted by some, to-morrow we are repelled by some. The same law cannot be applied at all times and in all cases. "Religion is the highest place of human thought and life, and herein the workings of these two forces have been most marked." At the outset, it apparently appears that there cannot reign unbroken harmony in this plane of mighty struggle. In every religion there are three parts, namely, philosophy, mythology and rituals. Every recognised religion [has] all these three things. But there can be no universal philosophy, mythology and rituals for the whole world. Where then the universality? How is it possible then to have a universal form of religion? "We all hear," says Swami Vivekananda,

> about universal brotherhood, and how societies stand up practically to preach this, Universal brotherhood, that is, we shout like drunken men we are all equal, therefore, let us make a sect. As soon as you make a sect you protest against equality, and thus it is no more. (Cf. the American lecture, delivered January 12, 1896 (Complete Works, II: 379-80).)

Mahomedans talk of universal brotherhood, but what comes out of them in reality? Nobody who is not a Mahomedan will be admitted into the brotherhood, he will have his throat cut. We think we cannot do better than quote his own words, wherein he with his wonderful lucidity and depth of views and in a remarkably catholic mind propounds forcibly the philosophy of the universal religion [*Vide* Complete Works, II: 375-96]. . . .

In society there are various natures of men. Some are active working men, there is the emotional man, then there is the mystic man and lastly there is the philosopher. Vivekananda strikes the key note of his whole philosophy when he declares that the attempt to help mankind to become beautifully balanced in all these four directions, is his ideal of religion and this religion is called in India, Yoga. The worker is called the Karma-yogin; who seeks union through love is called Bhakti-yogin; he who seeks through mysticism is called Raja-yogin; and he who seeks it through philosophy is called Jnan[a]-yogin. The religion which has a place for men of all these natures and a religion which satisf[ies] the thirst of men of different inclination, may be the universal religion, and that religion is Vedanta. Most cordially we recommend this admirable little book to our readers. For it contains some clear and definite expressions of views on the most vital problem that is engaging the serious attention of theologians. The price of the book is As. 3, and may be had at the Brahmavadin Office, Triplicane, Madras.

The Banquet For Ranjit Sinjhi

(*New Discoveries*, Vol. 4, pp. 479-80.)

[*The Indian Mirror*, December 16, 1896]

On the 21st of this month [November], the Cambridge "Indian Majlis" gave a complimentary dinner at the University Arms Hotel [in Cambridge] to Prince Ranjit-sinhji and Mr. Atul Chandra Chatterjee. Mr. Hafiz G. Sarwir of St. John's College, took the chair. There were about fifty Indians present and a few Englishmen. . . .

Swami Vivekananda rose next to respond [to the toast of India] amidst loud and deafening cheers. (There is no verbatim transcript available. Cf. the following January 8, 1897 Indian newspaper report, "The Majlis in Cambridge".) The Swami began by saying that he did not know exactly why he should be chosen to respond to the toast unless it be for the reason that he in physical bulk bore a striking resemblance to the national animal of India (laughter). He desired to congratulate the guest of the evening and he took the statement which the Chairman had made that Mr. Chatterjee was going to correct the mistake of past historians of India, to be literally true. For out of the past the future must come and he knew no greater and more permanent foundation for the future than a true knowledge of what had preceded before. The present is the effect of the infinity of causes which represent the past. They had many things to learn from the Europeans but their past, the glory of India which had passed away, should constitute even a still greater source of inspiration and instruction. Things rise and things decay, there is rise and fall everywhere in the world. . . . [*Vide* the block quotation under "The Majlis In Cambridge" for the remaining text of this report.]

The Majlis In Cambridge

(Vivekananda in Indian Newspapers, pp. 310-11.)

[The Amrita Bazar Patrika, January 8, 1897]

. . . The gathering was a unique one, for the Indians met together t talk (in the Majlis they all talk), about the successes of Ranjit Sing[h] an Atul Chandra Chatterjee. It is a pity the name of Professor Bose was nc associated with the above two; and we think, Swami Vivekananda, who wa present on the occasion, also deserved a recognition. We shall, however, nc commit the mistake of omitting the last two in noticing to show what th Indians have been able to achieve in the West.

What the Swamiji did was to remove the impression from the mind of the Americans that the Indians were barbarians, superstitious in the beliefs, and addicted to monstrous cruelties. The advent of the Swamiji i the West has done this service, that it has created an impression in man quarters that the Indians are not an inferior race as Sir Charles Elliot calle them, and that they can, in such subjects as religion and philosophy sa things which are not known even to the West. The advent of the Swami in the West has undoubtedly enhanced the character of the Indians in th West. . . .

Said Swami Vivekananda:—

> And though India is fallen to-day she will assuredly rise again. There was a time when India produced great philosophers and still greater prophets and preachers. The memory of those days ought to fill them with hope and confidence. This was not the first time in the history of India that they were so low. Periods of depression and degradation had occurred before this but India had always triumphed in the long run and so would she once again in the future. (At this time, there is no complete verbatim transcript available. Cf. the preceding December 16, 1896 Indian newspaper report , "The Banquet to Ranjit Sinhji", p.541.)

. . . . . .

Vivekananda In The West

(Vivekananda in Indian Newspapers, p. 312.)

[The Amrita Bazar Patrika, January 20, 1897]

Swami Vivekananda has received the ovation of a conquering hero, returning home. The last we heard of him in England was when he got a farewell address from his English disciples, who expressed their undying love for India. . . .

No one has any accurate knowledge of what Swami Vivekananda was doing in the West. We hear that he has made some impression in America and also in England. . . .

The Swami is, however, well aware of the nature of the mission before him. He says that Vedantism teaches the truth, which is that man is a divine being and that the highest and the lowest are the manifestations of the same Lord. He does not, however, admit that knowledge alone is sufficient for the salvation of man. Says he:—

> But his knowledge ought not to be a theory, but life. Religion is a realization, not talk, not doctrines, nor theories, however beautiful all these may be. Religion is being and becoming, not hearing or acknowledging. It is not an intellectual assent; but one's whole nature becoming changed into it. Such is religion. By an intellectual assent we can come to a hundred sort of foolish things, and change the next day, but this being and becoming is what is religion.

In the above noble sentiments, the Swami shews [shows] that he understands the situation pretty well. That which produces the rebirth of a man is religion. Under the influence of religion a man becomes a quite different being from what he was before. Unless that is the result of his religion, his religion is a myth.

. . . . . .

Bhakti*

(Vivekananda in Indian Newspapers, pp. 203-4.)

[*The Indian Mirror*, February 24, 1898]

Swami Vivekananda has been urging on the people of Lahore an Sialkote the need of practical work. (Cf. "Bhakti" (a report from The Tribune Complete Works, III: 391, for a somewhat different paraphrased passage The starving millions, he urged, cannot live on metaphysical speculatio they require bread; and in a lecture he gave at Lahore on Bhakti, h suggested as the best religion for to-day that everyman should, according his means, go out into the street and search for hungry Narayans, take the into their houses, feed them and clothe them. The giver should give to ma remembering that he is the highest temple of God. He had seen charity many countries, and the reason of its failure was the spirit, in which it wa carried out. "Here take this and go away". Charity belied its name so lor as it was given to gain reputation or applause of the world.

Our Mission In America

(*Vivekananda in Indian Newspapers, p. 208.*)

[*The Indian Mirror*, April 24, 1898]

Swami Vivekananda, in introducing the lecturer Swami Saradananda, said:

> Ladies and Gentlemen, — The speaker of tonight just comes from America. As you all know here that America is for your country, although our countrymen, specially Swami Dayananda Saraswati, used to call this country as *Patal*, inhabited by Laplands, Rakshas and Asurs, &c. (Laughter and loud cheers). Well, Gentlemen, whether it is *Patal* or not you ought to decide that by seeing those few ladies present here, who have come from the country of your so-called *Patal*, whether they are *Naga Kanyas* or not. (Cheers). Now, America is perfectly a new country. It was discovered by Columbus, the Italian, and before that a prior claim is put forward by the Norwegians who say, that they have discovered the northern part of it, and then before that there is another prior claim of the Chinese, who at one time preached the noble doctrine of Buddhism in all parts of the world, and it is said that Buddhist Missionaries were also sent from India to America, and specially in Washington, where some sort[s] of records are still to be traced by any traveller going there. Well, the table has now been turned at last for a century or more and instead of America being discovered, she discovers persons that go over to her. (Loud applause). It is a phenomenon that we observe every day there, multitudes of persons coming over from every part of the country [world?] and getting themselves discovered in the United States. It is a fact, well-known to you here all that several of our own countrymen have been discovered in that way. (Cheers). To-day, here I present before you one of your Calcutta boys, that has been similarly discovered by the Americans. (Cheers).

Swami Vivekananda [On Education] At Belur

(*Vivekananda in Indian Newspapers, p. 215.*)

[*The Indian Mirror*, February 15, 1901]

A correspondent writes: – "The following is an epitome of Swan Vivekananda's speech made in Belur M.E. School on the prize-distributic day held on the 22nd instant, Sunday, when the Swami was invited preside. The audience was composed chiefly of the boys of the school an some elderly gentlemen of Belur."

> The modern student is not practical. He is quite helpless. What our students want is not so much muscularity of body as hardihood. They are wanting in self-help. They are not accustomed to use their eyes and hands. No handicraft is taught. The present system of English education is entirely literary. The student must be made to think for himself and work for himself. Suppose there is a fire. He is the first to come forward and put on [out] the fire who is accustomed to use his eyes and hands. There is much truth in the criticism of Europeans touching the laziness of the Bengali, the slipshod way of his doing things. This can be soon remedied if the students be made to learn some handicraft apart from its utilitarian aspect, it is an education in itself.
>
> Secondly, how many thousands of students I know who live upon the worst food possible, and live amidst the most horrible surroundings, what wonder that there are so many idiots, imbeciles and cowards among them. They die like flies. The education that is given is onesided, weakening, it is killing by inches. The children are made to cram too much of useless matter, and are incarcerated in school rooms fifty or seventy in each, five hours together. They are given bad food. It is forgotten that the future health of the man is in the child. It is forgotten that nature can never be cheated and things cannot be pushed too early. In giving education to a child the law of growth has to be obeyed. And we must learn to wait. Nothing is more important

than that the child must have a strong and healthy body. The body is the first thing to attain to virtue. I know we are the poorest nation in the world, and we cannot afford to do much. We can only work on the lines of least resistance. We should see at least that our children are well fed. The machine of the child's body should never be exhausted. In Europe and America a man with crores of rupees sends his son if sickly, to the farmers, to till the ground. After three years he returns to the father healthy, rosy and strong. Then he is fit to be sent to school. We ought not for these reasons push the present system of education any further.

Thirdly, our character has disappeared. Our English education has destroyed everything and left nothing in its place. Our children have lost their politeness. To talk nicely is degrading. To be reverential to one's elders is degrading. Irreverence has been the sign of liberty. It is high time that we go back to our old politeness. The reformers have nothing to give in place of what they have taken away. Yet in spite of the most adverse surrounding of climate, etc., we have been able to do much, we have to do much more. I am proud of my race, I do not despair, I am seeing daily a glorious and wonderful future in my menial [mental] visions. Take greatest care of these young ones on whom our future depends.

Hindu Windows*

(Vivekananda in Indian Newspapers, p. 458.)

[The Indian Social Reformer, June 16, 1901]

A question having arisen in America as to the Swami Vivekananda's attitude towards social questions, a lady writes to an American paper as follows: "In one of his lectures at the Pouch Mansion, (Probably "India's Gift to the World", delivered February 25, 1895, of which there is no verbatim transcript available. Cf. two American newspaper articles published in Complete Works, II: 510-14 for somewhat different reports of this issue.) he spoke of the Hindu widows, declaring it unjust to state that they were generally subjected to cruelty or oppression in the Indians [*sic*] homes. He admitted that the prejudice against remarriage, and the custom which makes the widow a member of the husband's family instead of that of her own parents inflicted some hardships upon widows in India, and favoured wise efforts for their education which would render them self-supporting and in this way alleviate their condition. He emphasised his desire for the education and elevation of the women of his country, including the widows, by volunteering to give the entire proceeds of one of his lectures in support of the school of Babu Sasipada Banerjee, at Baranagar, near Calcutta, the institution of which preceded that of the Pandita Ramabai, at Poona, and where, if I am not mistaken, the Pandita herself obtained the first inspiration of her work. This lecture was given, and the proceeds were forwarded to Babu Sasipada Banerjee, and duly acknowledged."